Learn all the key facts with CGP!

Want to remember all the crucial facts for AQA GCSE Geography?
This CGP Knowledge Organiser is here to help!

We've condensed every topic down to the vital definitions,
facts and diagrams, making it all easy to memorise.

To check you've really got your facts straight, there's also a matching
Knowledge Retriever book that'll test you on every page.

CGP — still the best! ☺

Our sole aim here at CGP is to produce the highest quality books —
carefully written, immaculately presented and dangerously close to being funny.

Then we work our socks off to get them out to you
— at the cheapest possible prices.

Contents

Geographical Applications & Skills

Geographical Applications

Geographical Skills

Published by CGP.
Based on the classic CGP style created by Richard Parsons.

Editors: Claire Boulter, Tom Carney, Katherine Faudemer, Sharon Keeley-Holden, Becca Lakin.
Contributor: Paddy Gannon.

With thanks to Nic Robinson for the proofreading.
With thanks to Lottie Edwards for the copyright research.

ISBN: 978 1 78908 721 5

Printed by Elanders Ltd, Newcastle upon Tyne.
Clipart from Corel®

Natural Hazards

Two Types of Natural Hazard

NATURAL HAZARD — natural process which can threaten people / property.

1 Geological hazards — caused by land / tectonic processes, e.g. earthquakes.

2 Meteorological hazards — caused by weather / climate, e.g. tropical storms.

Three Hazard Risk Factors

HAZARD RISK — the probability of people being affected by a hazard.

1 Vulnerability: **More people in a hazardous area.** ⟹ Higher risk

2 Capacity to Cope: **More developed areas have better resources.** ⟹ Lower risk

3 Nature of Hazard:

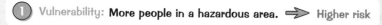

- **Type** — some hazards can be predicted / monitored. ⟹ Lower risk
- **Magnitude** — severe hazards have greater effects. ⟹ Higher risk
- **Frequency** — some hazards occur more often. ⟹ Higher risk

Effects

Primary effects → immediate impacts caused by hazards. E.g.

- Deaths and injuries
- Buildings destroyed
- Contaminated water supplies
- Damaged infrastructure
- Damaged crops

Secondary effects **happen later, often as a result of primary effects.** E.g.

- Other hazards, e.g. tsunamis
- Diseases from poor sanitation
- Shortages of food and clean water
- Weakened economy

Responses

Immediate responses **happen just before, during or right after hazards.** E.g.

- Evacuate people
- Seek / send aid
- Provide food, drink and shelter
- Rescue and treat injured
- Supply temporary gas / electricity

Long-term responses **deal with longer term effects.** E.g.

- Re-home people
- Restore water / gas / electricity
- Boost economy, e.g. with tourism
- Improve hazard management

Tectonic Plates

Tectonic Plates

TECTONIC PLATES — slabs of the Earth's crust that float on top of the mantle.

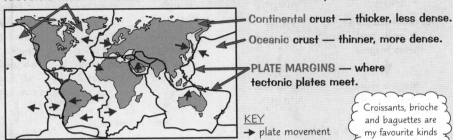

Continental crust — thicker, less dense.

Oceanic crust — thinner, more dense.

PLATE MARGINS — where tectonic plates meet.

KEY
→ plate movement

Croissants, brioche and baguettes are my favourite kinds of continental crust.

Three Types of Plate Margin

1 DESTRUCTIVE

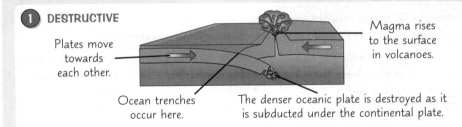

Plates move towards each other.

Magma rises to the surface in volcanoes.

Ocean trenches occur here.

The denser oceanic plate is destroyed as it is subducted under the continental plate.

2 CONSTRUCTIVE

Plates move away from each other.

Magma cools to create new crust.

Magma rises to fill the gap.

3 CONSERVATIVE

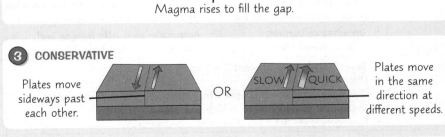

Plates move sideways past each other.

OR

SLOW   QUICK

Plates move in the same direction at different speeds.

Tectonic Hazards

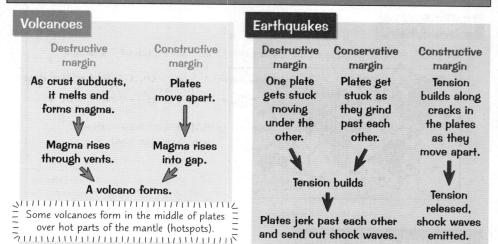

Volcanoes

Destructive margin	Constructive margin
As crust subducts, it melts and forms magma.	Plates move apart.
↓	↓
Magma rises through vents.	Magma rises into gap.

↘ ↙

A volcano forms.

Some volcanoes form in the middle of plates over hot parts of the mantle (hotspots).

Earthquakes

Destructive margin	Conservative margin	Constructive margin
One plate gets stuck moving under the other.	Plates get stuck as they grind past each other.	Tension builds along cracks in the plates as they move apart.

↘ ↙

Tension builds

↓

Plates jerk past each other and send out shock waves.

Tension released, shock waves emitted.

Living With Tectonic Hazards

People live in areas vulnerable to tectonic hazards for many reasons:

- They can't afford to move.
- They don't know the risks.
- They've always lived in the area.
- They think the government will support them.
- Management strategies can minimise risk.
- Volcanic ash makes soil fertile.
- Volcanoes attract tourists, creating jobs.

Management Strategies

	Volcanoes	Earthquakes
Monitoring and Prediction	• Scientists monitor changes in volcano shape, escaping gas and small earthquakes. • Helps predict eruptions.	Seismometers and lasers monitor tectonic plate movements → early warning systems.
Protection	• Strengthened / sloped roofs to withstand ash fall. • Trenches or barriers built to divert lava.	• New buildings use reinforced concrete. • Steel frames reinforce existing structures. • Automatic shut-offs for gas and electricity prevent fires.
Planning	• Teach people how to react if a hazard occurs. • Plan evacuation routes. • Stockpile emergency supplies (e.g. food, blankets, clean water). • Avoid new developments in high-risk areas. • Emergency services practise rescue procedures.	

Tectonic Hazards

Effects of Two Earthquakes

Both earthquakes were 7.8 magnitude.

	Kaikoura, New Zealand, 2016 (HIC)	Gorkha, Nepal, 2015 (LIC)
Primary effects	• 2 deaths, 50 injured. • US $8.5 billion damage. • 60 people → emergency housing. • Roads and railways destroyed. • Water, sewerage and power supplies cut off.	• 9000 deaths, 22 000 injured. • US $5 billion damage. • 800 000 buildings damaged. • 4 million people homeless. • Roads and bridges destroyed. • 2 million without clean water.
Secondary effects	• 100 000 landslides blocked roads and railways. • Clarence River blocked — flooding, 10 farms evacuated. • Tsunami with 5 m waves.	• Everest avalanches → 18 killed. • Landslides blocked roads which delayed aid. • Typhus outbreaks → 13+ killed.

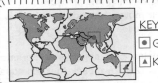

KEY
- ● Gorkha
- ▲ Kaikoura

Responses to Two Earthquakes

	Kaikoura, New Zealand, 2016 (HIC)	Gorkha, Nepal, 2015 (LIC)
Immediate responses	• Tsunami warning issued. • Hundreds in emergency shelters. • Vulnerable people evacuated by helicopter. • Power restored within hours. • Temporary water supplies set up. • Other countries sent food and medicine.	• Efforts to rescue people slowed by lack of tools. • Bodies recovered and injured people treated. • 130 000 families housed in emergency shelters. • Charities provided aid, but delivery was slowed by blocked roads.
Long-term responses	• $5.3m from District Council for repairs and rebuilding. • Road and rail routes reopened within 2 years. • Relief fund set up to provide basic supplies. • Earthquake-proof water main laid.	• $500m from World Bank Group. • Some roads reopened. • Heritage sites reopened in June 2015 to attract tourists. • Water supplies restored but took a long time. • NGOs working with residents to increase disaster resilience.

Global Atmospheric Circulation

Global Atmospheric Circulation Model

GLOBAL ATMOSPHERIC CIRCULATION — the transfer of heat from the equator to the poles by the movement of air.

Sun warms equator. Air rises, forming a low pressure belt, then cools and moves away.

At 30° N and S, cool air sinks, creating a high pressure belt. It moves back towards equator (trade winds) or towards the poles (westerlies).

At 60° N and S, warmer surface air rises, creating low pressure. Some air moves towards equator. The rest moves towards the poles.

At the poles, cool air sinks and creates high pressure. Air flows back towards equator.

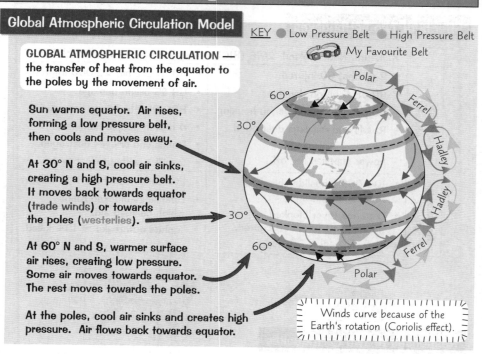

KEY ● Low Pressure Belt ● High Pressure Belt
🥽 My Favourite Belt

Polar
Ferrel
Hadley
Hadley
Ferrel
Polar

60°
30°
30°
60°

Winds curve because of the Earth's rotation (Coriolis effect).

Weather Impacts

Equator:
Sun directly overhead → hot
Warm, moist air rises → rainy

30° N and S:
Moisture already
released → low rainfall

60° N and S:
Warm rising air →
cloudy and rainy

Atmospheric Circulation and Tropical Storm Formation

TROPICAL STORMS — low pressure systems with intense wind and rain.

• Between 5° and 30° N and S   • Sea temperature ≥ 27 °C   • Low wind shear

Warm water evaporates, rises and condenses, producing energy. ➡ Low pressure drives surface winds. ➡ Easterly winds move tropical storms west. ➡ Storms strengthen as they move over warm water.

The Coriolis effect makes storms rotate.

Storms lose energy moving over land / cold water.

Unit 1A — The Challenge of Natural Hazards

Tropical Storms

Features of Tropical Storms

Risks include strong winds, heavy rain and storm surges.

Circular shape

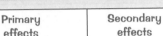

← 300 km →

Eyewall — spiralling rising air, very strong winds, storm clouds, torrential rain, lower temperature

Eye — low pressure, light wind, no clouds, no rain, higher temperature

West ← → East

At the storm's edge — lighter wind, smaller and scattered clouds, lighter rain, warmer.

Typhoon Haiyan — Philippines, 2013

Primary effects	Secondary effects	Immediate responses	Long-term responses
• 8000 people killed. • 1 million homes severely damaged. • Electricity lines destroyed. • Water contaminated. • 600 000 hectares of farmland flooded.	• Flooding triggered landslides. • 5.6 million jobs lost. • Outbreaks of disease, e.g. dysentery.	• 800 000 evacuated. • Charities gave food, shelter and clean water. • Pit latrines built for 100 000 people.	• UN raised $300 million for rebuilding. • Storm-resistant houses built. • Tourists urged to visit.

Flooding / deaths caused by storm surge.

Reducing Tropical Storm Effects

Prediction and Monitoring	Planning	Protection
• Radar, satellites and aircraft monitor storms. • Computer models predict storm paths.	• Future developments avoid high-risk areas. • Evacuation routes planned. • Emergency services practise rescue procedures.	• Buildings designed to withstand storms. • Buildings put on stilts. • Flood defences built.

Climate Change and Tropical Storms

Distribution: Larger ocean area above 27 °C ⇒ Tropical storms at higher latitudes

Frequency: Oceans above 27 °C for longer ⇒ More time for tropical storms to form

Intensity: More evaporation and more cloud ⇒ More powerful tropical storms

UK Weather Hazards

Types of UK Weather Hazards

Strong winds	Property damage. Transport disruption. Uprooted trees and debris can kill people.
Heavy rainfall	Flooding damages homes, disrupts transport and can drown people. Recovery can cost millions.
Snow and ice	People slip on ice or die from cold-related illnesses.
Drought	Crop failure. Rules introduced to conserve water.
Thunderstorms	Strong wind and heavy rain (see above). Lightning can cause fires.
Heat waves	Pollution builds up. People suffer from heat exhaustion or breathing difficulties. Roads melt and rails buckle. Tourism may benefit.

Extreme Weather

The UK's weather is becoming more extreme.

 Seven of eleven coldest temperatures on record occurred since 1980. Dec. 2010 — coldest month in 100 years.

 Ten warmest years all since 1990.

 2010-2014 — Many rainfall records broken.

Major flooding events more frequent over the past decade.

Somerset Levels Flooding — Dec. 2013-Feb. 2014

 EXAMPLE

Causes	Impacts	Management
Physical: • 3x avg. monthly rainfall during winter 2013-2014. • Rain fell on saturated, low-lying ground. • High tides and storm surges. **Human:** • Rivers hadn't been dredged regularly for 20 yrs.	**Social:** • 600 homes flooded. • Villages cut off. • Transport links disrupted. • Insurance prices soared. **Economic:** • £80m damage. • Businesses lost £1.2m. • £200m tourism lost. **Environmental:** • 11 500 hectares flooded. • Crops destroyed. • Standing water made ground toxic. • Loss of soil fertility. • Mud damaged vegetation	**Before:** • People told to find emergency accommodation. • Sandbags and flood boards protected homes. **After:** Flood Action Plan. £100m to: • Make temporary pumping stations permanent. • Regularly dredge rivers Parrett and Tone. • Widen River Sowy and King's Sedgemoor Drain. • Build tidal barrage at Bridgwater.

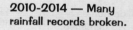

Climate Change

Evidence for Climate Change

CLIMATE CHANGE — any significant change in the Earth's climate over a long period.

During the Quaternary period (the last 2.6 million years), Earth has shifted between glacial periods (cold) and interglacial periods (warmer).

Ice cores	Sediment cores	Tree rings	Pollen analysis	Temperature records
Gases trapped in layers of ice show temperature change.	Remains of organisms in ocean sediments show past conditions.	Thicker rings mean warmer, wetter conditions.	Preserved pollen shows tree types and past climate.	Accurate measurements since 1850s. Historical records extend further back.

Three Natural Causes

 Orbital changes affect how much of the Sun's energy reaches Earth.

MORE ENERGY ⟹ MORE WARMING

elliptical orbit

Sun

circular orbit

Wobble of Earth's axis varies.

Stretch — shape of Earth's orbit varies.

Tilt of Earth's axis varies.

 Volcanic eruptions eject material into atmosphere.

⬇

Sun's rays reflected.

⬇

Earth's surface cools temporarily.

 Solar output changes in 11 year cycles.

⬇

Reduced energy = cooler areas.

Four Human Causes

Global warming is the sharp rise in temp. over the last century.

GREENHOUSE EFFECT — greenhouse gases absorb outgoing heat from the Earth.

Increased greenhouse gas emissions → planet warms

 Fossil fuels: Release CO_2 when burnt.

 Cement production: Turning limestone into cement releases CO_2.

Farming: Livestock and rice paddies emit methane.

Deforestation: When trees are cut down, they stop storing CO_2.

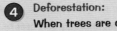 CO_2 CO_2 CO_2 CO_2

Climate Change

Effects of Climate Change

Wet places will get wetter. Dry places will get drier.

ENVIRONMENTAL	HUMAN
• Glaciers and ice sheets melt → sea level rises. • Shrinking sea ice → loss of polar habitat. • Flooding of low-lying, coastal areas → loss of coastal habitats. • Changing precipitation patterns. • Species are declining, e.g. coral reefs bleached. • Species moving to higher latitudes. • Habitat damage making species extinct → declining biodiversity.	• More deaths due to heat. • Fewer deaths due to cold. • People leave uninhabitable areas → overcrowding in other areas. • Decreased rainfall in some areas → limited water availability. • Lower crop yields globally → malnutrition, ill health and death. • High latitude crop yields may increase. • More extreme weather → management / rebuilding costs rise.

Management Strategies

MITIGATION aims to reduce the causes of climate change.

Alternative energy production:
Nuclear or renewable energy sources lower emissions.

Planting trees:
More trees = more CO_2 absorbed.

Carbon Capture and Storage:
CO_2 emissions from power stations stored securely.

International agreements:
Paris Agreement (2016) — countries pledged to reduce greenhouse gas emissions.

ADAPTATION responds to the effects of climate change.

Changing Agricultural Systems:
• **Plant crops suited to changed climates.**
• **Biotechnology can create drought-resistant crops.**

Managing Water Supply:
• **Water meters help limit water use.**
• **Rainwater and waste water collected and recycled.**

Coping with Rising Sea Levels:
• **Better flood warning systems and flood defences, e.g. Thames Barrier.**
• **Build houses on embankments, build raised flood shelters.**

Ecosystems

Key Definitions

ECOSYSTEM — All the biotic (living) and abiotic (non-living) parts of an area.

- PRODUCERS produce food from sunlight.
- CONSUMERS eat other organisms for energy.
- DECOMPOSERS break down dead material for energy.

Nutrient Cycle

Plants absorb nutrients from soil.

Animals eat plants.

Plants drop leaves.

Plants and animals decompose.

Small-scale Ecosystem — Slapton Ley Reed Beds, UK

EXAMPLE

Common reed — main producer

Water voles and moth larvae eat reeds.

Dragonflies lay eggs.

Eels use reeds for shelter.

Frogs and fish eat insect larvae.

Birds eat seedheads.

Herons nest in reed beds and eat eels and frogs.

Reed roots bind soil, preventing erosion.

Bacteria decompose dead organic matter.

Food chains show what eats what. ➡ Common reed → Moth larva → Eel → Heron

Food webs show how food chains overlap. ➡ Common reed

Moth larva → Dragonfly larva → Eel

Water beetle → Dragonfly → Frog → Heron

Changes can affect interdependent organisms, e.g.

Drought dries up pools ➡ Insect larvae die ➡ Fish and frog numbers decrease ➡ Heron numbers decline

Global Ecosystems

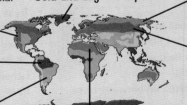

Polar — Cold and dry. Few plants.

Temperate Deciduous Forest — Four distinct seasons. Mild and damp.

Tropical Rainforest — Hot and wet. Lush forest.

Grassland — Savannah (wet and dry seasons) or temperate (dry).

Tundra — Cold winters and brief summers. Moss and grass.

Boreal Forest — Cold, dry winters. Mild, wet summers. Coniferous trees.

Hot Desert — Very dry. Large temperature range. Sparse plants.

Tropical Rainforests

Characteristics

Climate	No definite seasons. Sun directly overhead → Hot. High daily rainfall.
Plants	Evergreen plants take advantage of continual growing season. Tall trees and dense vegetation → dark forest floor. Epiphytes grow on other plants.
Soil	Rain washes nutrients away → Not very fertile. Fallen leaves decay quickly.
People	Indigenous people have adapted → hunt, fish, forage and farm.
Animals	More species than any other ecosystem.

> Rainforest animals: sloths, jaguars, anacondas, gorillas, tree frogs.

Biodiversity

BIODIVERSITY — the variety of organisms living in a particular area.

Constant climate ⇒ Productive, stable environment ⇒ Plants and animals not threatened by change ⇒ HIGH biodiversity

But:

Deforestation / human development ⇒ Change imposed on species who can't adapt ⇒ Extinction of some species ⇒ LOSS of biodiversity

Interdependence

Surface soil high in nutrients.
↗ ↘
Warm / wet climate → fast decomposition.   Plants grow easily.
↖ ↙
Plants / animals die. ⇐ Animals eat plants for nutrients.

Human activity affects ecosystem:

Trees cut down.
↓
Soil less protected.
↓
Rain washes nutrients away.
↓
Plants struggle to grow.

Adaptations

ANIMALS

- Sharp sense of smell to cope with dark forest floor.
- Nocturnal animals feed at night to save energy.
- Short wings help birds fly between trees.
- Many animals can swim to cross rivers.
- Camouflage to hide from predators.

> Hmmm... jaguar with a hint of sloth.

PLANTS

- Trees are tall to reach sunlight.
- Waxy drip-tips for easy runoff.
- Lianas climb trees for light.
- Buttress roots support tall trees.

Emergent Trees
Main Canopy
Undercanopy
Shrub layer

Tropical Rainforests — Deforestation

CASE STUDY

Causes of Deforestation in The Amazon

Commercial Farming 250 000 km² cleared to produce soy.
200 million cattle on 450 000 km² of pasture.

Subsistence Farming Small-scale farmers grow crops for family.

Logging Hardwood trees tempt legal and illegal loggers.

Mineral Extraction
Mining gold, iron ore and copper boosts development. Explosives used.

Road Building
Trans-Amazonian Highway threatens to open up remote areas.

Population Growth
Land offered to poor people from overcrowded cities.

Energy Development
Balbina Dam flooded 2400 km² of forest.

70-80%
20-25%
2-3%
<2%

Percentages of total deforestation in the Amazon.

Almost 18 million hectares of forest were lost between 2001 and 2012.

Three Impacts of Deforestation in the Amazon

1 CLIMATE CHANGE: 140 billion tonnes of carbon stored in the Amazon → Felling trees releases some of this as CO_2 → Global warming

2 SOIL EROSION:
Fewer trees → Less rain absorbed / intercepted ↘ More nutrients wash away
↑ ↙
Farmers clear more land ← Reduced soil fertility

3 ECONOMIC CHANGE:
- Loss of rubber trees → Brazilian rubber tappers lose jobs.
- Buenaventura mining company (Peru) → 8000 employees.
- Brazil exported $600 million of beef in March 2018.

Wealth and jobs boost development but can destroy resources.

Changing Rates of Deforestation

Deforestation in Brazil reduced by 80% from 2004 to 2012.

Global rates of deforestation are high and generally increasing, but some countries (e.g. Brazil) are trying to reduce this:

- Increased global awareness reduces demand for products from deforested areas.
- Paris Agreement — Brazil pledged to reduce emissions 37% by 2025.
- Satellite imagery prevents large-scale illegal logging.
- Funding now protects 44% of the Amazon.

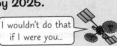
I wouldn't do that if I were you...

Tropical Rainforests and Sustainability

Tropical Rainforests — Value

- Source of many products and medicines — some may still be undiscovered.
- Sustainable development → long-term economic benefits (e.g. ecotourism).
- Rainforests may reduce the greenhouse effect (trees absorb CO_2).
- Regulation of climate and water cycle
  → deforestation increases risk of drought or flooding.

Deforestation could affect all countries (e.g. climate change) not just deforested areas.

Sustainable Management Strategies

SUSTAINABLE MANAGEMENT — getting the resources we need today without damaging the environment so that resources aren't available in the future.

Replanting
- New trees (of the same type) replace felled ones.
- A legal requirement for logging companies in certain countries.

 Selective Logging
- Some trees felled but most remain.
- Forest can regenerate.
→ Malaysia — helicopter logging.

Ecotourism
- Small groups of tourists follow strict environmental rules.
- Locals hired → less need for them to mine, farm or log for income.
- Incentive to conserve environment.
→ 21% of Costa Rica protected from development for ecotourism.

 Education
- Encourages sustainable product use.
- Teaches locals to make money in an environmentally-friendly way.
→ Rainforest Alliance teaches communities in Guatemala about sustainable living.

Conservation
- National parks / nature reserves restrict damaging activities.
- Countries can set up funds for overseas investors to donate to.
→ 2018 — Norway paid $70m into Brazil's Amazon Fund.

 Reducing Debt
- Debt can be cancelled — countries don't have to log, farm or mine to repay it.
- Conservation swaps → countrie's debt paid off if conservation is guaranteed.
→ 2011 — USA reduced Indonesia's debt by $29m.

International Hardwood Agreements
- Prevent illegal logging.
- Promote the use of hardwood from sustainably-managed forests.
→ Forest Stewardship Council® mark on sustainably-sourced timber.

Hot Deserts

Characteristics

Climate	Very little rainfall. Few clouds → extreme heat (day) and extreme cold (night).
Plants	Low rainfall → few plants. Plants don't need much water, e.g. cacti. Plants are usually short. Short life cycles → quick growth after rain.
Soil	Lack of leaf fall → low fertility. Low rainfall → dry. Shallow and gravelly.
People	Live near water sources to grow crops. Nomadic → travel for food / water.
Animals	Adapted to harsh environment. Most mammals are small and nocturnal. Most birds leave during harshest conditions.

Biodiversity

Low biodiversity overall.

People threaten biodiversity:

- Desertification.
- Over-use and contamination of water supplies.
- Roads divide habitats → migrating animals threatened.
- Global warming makes deserts hotter and drier → species migrate or risk decline and extinction.

Deserts contain biodiversity hotspots — places with high proportions of endemic species at risk of extinction.

Interdependence

Hot desserts are often served with custard.

Hot, dry climate → high evaporation and little decomposition.

Fewer animals to die.

Soil salty and low in nutrients.

Low-density populations. ← Limited plant growth → low food supply.

Human activity affects fragile ecosystem:

Overgrazing cattle → soil erosion.

Loose soil → sand forms dust clouds.

Rainfall reduced → water supplies dry up.

People, plants and animals die.

Adaptations

PLANTS

- Long roots reach deep water supplies.
- Wide roots absorb rainwater.
- Succulents store water in large fleshy stems.
- Small leaves, spines and waxy skin reduce transpiration.
- Some seeds only germinate after rain.

ANIMALS

- Nocturnal → avoid hottest temps.
- Long limbs and large ears increase surface area → helps heat loss.
- Underground burrows → cooler.
- Camels store water in fat (humps).
- Minimised water loss → kangaroo rats don't sweat.

The Sahara and Desertification

Opportunities and Challenges in the Sahara

CASE STUDY

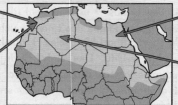

Small-scale tourism in desert. Many visit outskirts, e.g. Marrakesh.

Aswan Dam (Egypt) provides water for agriculture all year.

Morocco extracts many minerals, e.g. phosphate.

94% Algeria's exports from oil and gas industries.

12+ hours of sun → ideal for generating solar power.

	Extreme Temperatures	Limited Water Supply	Inaccessibility
Challenges to Development	• Extreme heat and cold is dangerous. • Seasonal tourism → few tourists in hot season. • Physical work (e.g. farming / mining) at high temps is difficult.	• Low, variable rainfall → providing water for industry is difficult. • Water pipes are expensive to build. • Deep boreholes extract water unsustainably.	• Difficult to provide services to remote communities. • Oil and gas pipelines are expensive to build. • Few roads / long distances to drive → air travel required.

Desertification

Areas on the edge of deserts are at risk of desertification.

DESERTIFICATION — degradation of land making it drier and less productive.

CAUSES:

 Overgrazing
Plants eaten faster than they regrow.

 Removal of fuel wood
Trees felled for fuel → soil exposed.

 Population growth
Land under pressure → impacts intensify.

 Over-cultivation
Continually planting crops in the same area depletes nutrients and erodes soil.

Climate change
Rising temps increase evaporation and decrease rainfall → plants die.

REDUCING DESERTIFICATION RISK			
Water management	Tree planting	Soil management	Appropriate technology
• Grow crops that don't need much water, e.g. olives. • Drip irrigation stops erosion.	Trees act as windbreaks, shade crops and stabilise sand.	• Rest land between grazing / planting to replenish nutrients. • Rotate crops so different nutrients are removed. • Add nutrients with compost.	Use cheap, sustainable, local materials, e.g. sand fences.

Polar and Tundra Environments

Characteristics

Polar areas can reach -90 °C. Tundra can reach -50 °C.

	Polar	Tundra
Climate	Very cold. Very low precipitation. Defined but cold seasons.	Cold. Low precipitation. Defined but cold seasons.
Plants	Few. Mosses and lichens. Grasses on the coast.	Hardy shrubs, grasses, mosses, lichens. Small short trees in warmer areas.
Soil	Covered by ice sheets → no exposed soil.	Thin, acidic, infertile. Permafrost layer traps greenhouse gases.
People	Mostly uninhabited.	Indigenous people. Oil and gas workers.
Animals	Polar bears, whales, penguins.	Lemmings, wolves and reindeer.

Biodiversity

Very low biodiversity → Change in one species affects all dependent species. ➡ Global warming → some species move to pole for colder temps. ➡ Polar species can't go anywhere colder. ➡ Some species at risk of decline or extinction.

Interdependence

Cold slows decomposition. ⟶ Few nutrients in soil.

Carnivores follow herbivores. ⬇ Limited plant growth. ⬇

⬆ Herbivores migrate to find food. ⬇

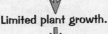

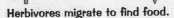
• Plants protect permafrost.
• Permafrost gives plants water.

Cold environments are very fragile.

If people trample plants, the exposed soil is warmed by sun. ⬇

Permafrost may melt & saturate soil → greenhouse gases released. ⬇

Plants can't grow, herbivores struggle to find food.

Adaptations

PLANTS

Zzzzzzz

• Plants become dormant to survive cold and dark winters.
• Low-growing / round-shaped → wind protection.
• Shallow roots above permafrost.
• Small leaves limit transpiration.
• Short growing season.

ANIMALS

• Fur or blubber keeps animals warm.
• Animals hibernate to conserve energy.
• Non-hibernators → adapted to survive on limited food sources.
• Birds migrate to warmer areas for winter.
• White winter coats — help predators stalk prey, help prey avoid predators.

Alaska and Sustainable Management

Opportunities and Challenges in Alaska

CASE STUDY

Energy	Mineral resources	Fishing	Tourism
Oil and gas — over half state's income. Trans-Alaska pipeline connects oil fields to Valdez.	Gold, silver, copper and iron ore mined. $154 million worth of gold exported in 2015.	2016 — fishing industry worth $1.7 billion and employed 30 000 fishermen.	2 million tourists bring in $2.5 billion each year and generate jobs for 39 000 people.

Inaccessibility
- Remote, mountainous areas → difficult to access.
- Air travel → expensive.
- Ice roads → dangerous.
- Some roads close in summer → ground too soft.
- Small, scattered population → far from jobs and services.

Extreme Temperatures
- Extreme cold is dangerous.
- Daylight hours vary a lot.

Barrow, Alaska gets 67 days of total darkness a year.

Buildings and Infrastructure
- Soft / frozen ground and extreme temp. makes construction expensive.
- Construction only happens in summer.
- Pipelines built on stilts to stop them melting permafrost.

Cold Environments — Value

WILDERNESS AREA — wild, natural environments that are undeveloped, uninhabited and undisturbed.

They need to be conserved because:

- they provide habitats for organisms that can't survive elsewhere.
- scientists can study areas relatively unaffected by people.
- knowledge allows conditions to be replicated in managed ecosystems → rare species preserved.
- they're extremely fragile.

Damaged plants take a long time to regrow. / Species are specialised → struggle to adapt to change.

Conservation & Development

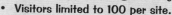

International Agreements
1959 Antarctica Treaty — tourism controlled to protect fragile ecosystem.
- Visitors limited to 100 per site.
- Peaceful non-military activities.
- Nuclear activity prohibited.
- Cruises with 500+ people can't stop.

 Role of Governments
Laws (e.g. 1964 Wilderness Act) can prevent development in wilderness areas → reduced conflict over land use.

Using Technology
Modern construction methods minimise environmental impacts → gravel beds stop heated buildings melting permafrost.

 Conservation Groups
These pressure governments to protect cold environments → more sustainable development.

The UK Physical Landscape

Upland and Lowland Areas in the UK

Upland areas — formed of hard, igneous (e.g. granite) and metamorphic (e.g. slate and schist) rocks that are resistant to erosion.

Lowland areas — formed of softer sedimentary rocks (e.g. chalk and clays) that erode more easily.

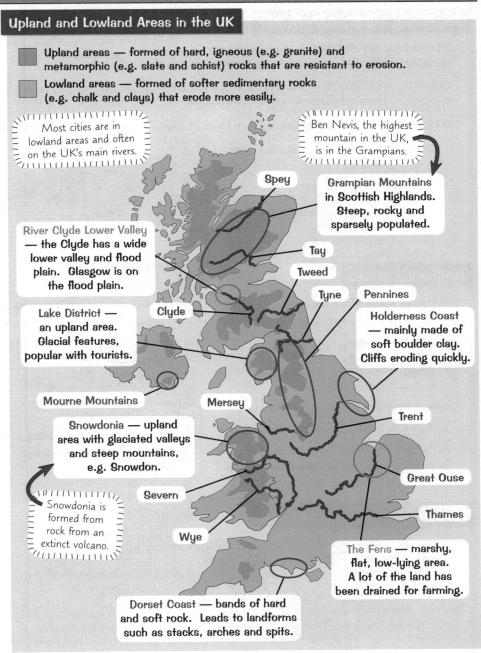

Most cities are in lowland areas and often on the UK's main rivers.

Ben Nevis, the highest mountain in the UK, is in the Grampians.

Spey

Grampian Mountains in Scottish Highlands. Steep, rocky and sparsely populated.

River Clyde Lower Valley — the Clyde has a wide lower valley and flood plain. Glasgow is on the flood plain.

Tay

Tweed

Tyne

Pennines

Clyde

Lake District — an upland area. Glacial features, popular with tourists.

Holderness Coast — mainly made of soft boulder clay. Cliffs eroding quickly.

Mourne Mountains

Mersey

Trent

Snowdonia — upland area with glaciated valleys and steep mountains, e.g. Snowdon.

Great Ouse

Snowdonia is formed from rock from an extinct volcano.

Severn

Thames

Wye

The Fens — marshy, flat, low-lying area. A lot of the land has been drained for farming.

Dorset Coast — bands of hard and soft rock. Leads to landforms such as stacks, arches and spits.

Coastal Processes

Weathering and Mass Movement

MECHANICAL WEATHERING — the breakdown of rock without changing its chemical composition, e.g. freeze-thaw weathering.

> Freezing and thawing water in cracks breaks rock up.

CHEMICAL WEATHERING — the breakdown of rock by changing its chemical composition, e.g. carbonation.

> Carbonic acid in rainwater dissolves rocks containing calcium carbonate.

MASS MOVEMENT — gravity acts on rock / loose material → material shifts down slope.

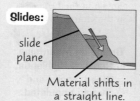

Slides:

slide plane

Material shifts in a straight line.

Slumps:

scarp

Material rotates along a curved slip plane.

Rockfalls:

bedding plane

Material breaks up and falls downslope.

Destructive Waves

Destructive waves erode the coast.

waves are high-frequency, high and steep

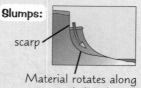

backwash > swash = material removed

Waves wear away the coast by:

- Hydraulic power (air forced into rock)
- Abrasion (scraping / rubbing of rock)
- Attrition (rocks collide, break and smooth)

Constructive Waves

Constructive waves deposit material.

waves are low frequency, low and long

swash > backwash = deposition

Deposition — waves lose energy and drop sediment when:

- rolling up beach & spreading out
- lots of material is transported into the area

Transportation — Longshore Drift

LONGSHORE DRIFT — gradual zig-zag movement of material along coast.

Waves follow wind direction.

Swash carries material up the beach.

Backwash carries material back down beach.

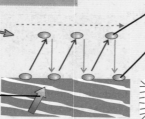

Water moves sediment by traction, suspension, saltation and solution.

Coastal Landforms

Landforms Caused by Deposition

BEACHES — formed by constructive waves.

SPITS — formed when longshore drift transports material past bend in coastline.

wind forms recurved end

area behind spit sheltered — material accumulates, plants grow

BARS — formed when a spit joins two headlands.

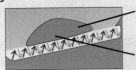

lagoon forms behind bar

bay cut off from the sea

SAND DUNES — formed when sand deposited by longshore drift is moved up beach by wind.

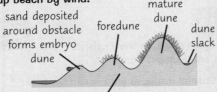

sand deposited around obstacle forms embryo dune

foredune

mature dune

dune slack

plants grow and more sand accumulates

Landforms Caused by Erosion

HEADLANDS and BAYS:

softer rock erodes faster to form a bay

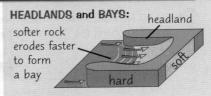

headland

soft

hard

CAVES, ARCHES and STACKS:

headland erosion over time

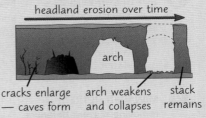

arch

cracks enlarge — caves form

arch weakens and collapses

stack remains

WAVE-CUT PLATFORMS:

1 Erosion causes wave-cut notch.

2 Rock above collapses.

3 New wave-cut notch.

4 Cliff retreats. wave-cut platform.

Rock type affects landform development. Coasts can be discordant or concordant.

HARD SOFT   SOFT HARD

Coastal Landscape — Dorset

EXAMPLE

Bands of hard and soft rock have eroded at different rates.

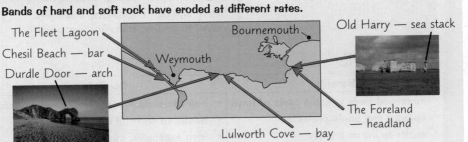

The Fleet Lagoon

Chesil Beach — bar

Durdle Door — arch

Weymouth

Bournemouth

Old Harry — sea stack

The Foreland — headland

Lulworth Cove — bay

Coastal Management

Management Strategies

1 **HARD ENGINEERING — man-made structures built to control the flow of the sea.**

Hard engineering — relatively cheap but can be ugly and need replacing.

sea wall

gabion

rock armour

groyne

longshore drift

reflects waves   absorbs wave energy — reduces erosion   traps material

2 **SOFT ENGINEERING — uses knowledge of the sea and its processes.**

Soft engineering — more sustainable but can be expensive.

beach nourishment and reprofiling

added material widens beach — slows waves

dune regeneration

plants stabilise dunes — dunes form barrier

3 **MANAGED RETREAT — removing current defences and allowing flooding.**

land becomes marshland — protects land behind from flooding and erosion

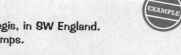

breach in old defences

Managed retreat is cheap and easy but may affect farmers.

UK Coastal Management — Lyme Regis

EXAMPLE

Powerful waves erode the sea cliffs around Lyme Regis, in SW England. Properties have been damaged by landslides and slumps.

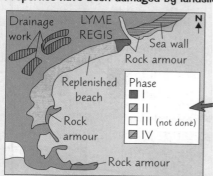

Drainage work
LYME REGIS
Sea wall
Rock armour
Replenished beach
Rock armour
Rock armour

Phase
■ I
▨ II
☐ III (not done)
▨ IV

Coastal management needed because:
- 3600+ residents in Lyme Regis.
- Local economy depends on tourism.
- 900 m of road would have been lost.

1990s-2015 — Four phases of work.

Hard and soft engineering strategies used to protect town from erosion.

Benefits	Conflicts
• increased trade in some parts of town	• more tourists = more traffic / litter / noise
• harbour and boats protected	• harder to find and excavate fossils
• easier to insure houses	• very expensive, may need rebuilding

The River Valley and Fluvial Processes

River Profiles

LONG PROFILE — shows gradient changes along river course.

CROSS PROFILE — shows what river cross-section looks like.

upland area

source

mouth

sea or lake

course	gradient	valley and channel shape	cross profile
upper	steep	V-shaped valley, steep sides. Narrow, shallow channel.	
middle	medium	Gently sloping valley sides. Wider, deeper channel.	
lower	gentle	Very wide, almost flat valley. Very wide, deep channel.	

Cross profile determined by type of erosion:

Vertical erosion — deepens river valley and channel, making it V-shaped. Dominant in upper course.

Lateral erosion — widens river valley and channel. Dominant in middle / lower courses.

Processes of Erosion

 HYDRAULIC ACTION — force of water breaks rock away from the river channel.

 ABRASION — eroded rocks scrape and wear away river channel.

 ATTRITION — Eroded rocks collide and break up / rub together and smooth edges.

 SOLUTION — some rocks dissolve, e.g. chalk.

Transportation of Eroded Material

TRACTION — large particles pushed along the river bed.

SALTATION — pebble-sized particles are bounced along the river bed.

SUSPENSION — small particles are carried along.

 SOLUTION — materials dissolve in the water and are carried along.

Deposition

DEPOSITION — when a river drops transported material.
Occurs when rivers lose velocity and energy. Rivers slow because:

Deposition is dominant in the lower course.

- The water is shallower.
- The river reaches its mouth.
- The volume of water falls.
- The amount of eroded material increases.

Smaller particles → transported further → deposited closer to river's mouth.

River Landforms

Landforms Resulting from Erosion

WATERFALLS and GORGES

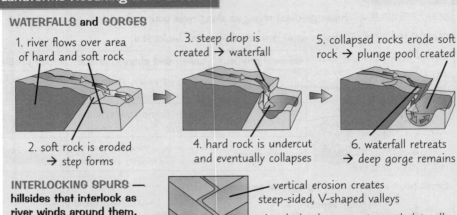

1. river flows over area of hard and soft rock

2. soft rock is eroded → step forms

3. steep drop is created → waterfall

4. hard rock is undercut and eventually collapses

5. collapsed rocks erode soft rock → plunge pool created

6. waterfall retreats → deep gorge remains

INTERLOCKING SPURS — hillsides that interlock as river winds around them.

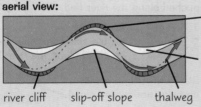

— vertical erosion creates steep-sided, V-shaped valleys

— river lacks the power to erode laterally → has to wind around hillsides

Landforms Resulting from Erosion and Deposition

Thalweg — line of deepest water and fastest flow.

MEANDERS — large bends in a river's middle or lower course.

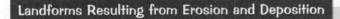

aerial view:

deeper outside bend = faster current → more erosion

shallower inside bend = slower current → more deposition

river cliff   slip-off slope   thalweg

cross-section:

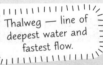
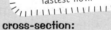

Oxbow lakes form on meanders.

OX-BOW LAKE — small horseshoe-shaped lake cut off from main river channel.

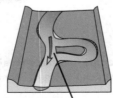

outside bends get closer, until only separated by small bit of land (the neck)

river breaks through (often during floods), flowing along new shortest course

deposition cuts off meander, forming ox-bow lake

River Landforms

Landforms Resulting from Deposition

FLOOD PLAINS — wide, flat valley floor on either side of a river that floods.

river floods ⟹ water slows down and loses energy ⟹ material deposited ⟹ flood plain builds up

Slip-off slopes of meanders also build up flood plains.

LEVEES — natural embankments along the edges of a river channel.

floods deposit material on flood plain

material builds up after repeated flooding → levees created

heaviest material deposited closest to channel

ESTUARIES — tidal areas where rivers meet the sea.

high tide:

low tide:

Water level rises and falls each day.

silt and sand deposited — build up creates mudflats

river channel

river mouth

mudflats exposed

The River Clyde

EXAMPLE

The River Clyde flows about 160 km through Scotland.

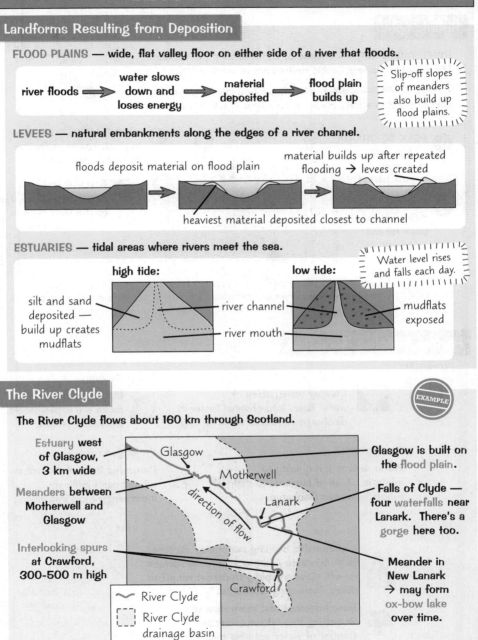

Estuary west of Glasgow, 3 km wide

Glasgow

Motherwell

Lanark

direction of flow

Meanders between Motherwell and Glasgow

Interlocking spurs at Crawford, 300-500 m high

Crawford

~ River Clyde

⌐ ¬ River Clyde
   drainage basin
∟ ⌐

Glasgow is built on the **flood plain**.

Falls of Clyde — four **waterfalls** near Lanark. There's a **gorge** here too.

Meander in New Lanark → may form **ox-bow lake** over time.

Flooding and Flood Management

Hydrographs

RIVER DISCHARGE — volume of water flowing per second. Measured in cumecs (cubic metres per second, m³/s).

HYDROGRAPH — a graph that shows how discharge at a certain point in a river changes over time in relation to rainfall.

a rising limb

1 PEAK DISCHARGE — highest discharge in time period

2 LAG TIME — delay between peak rainfall and peak discharge

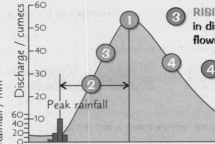

Peak rainfall

3 RISING LIMB — increase in discharge as rainwater flows into the river

4 FALLING LIMB — decrease in discharge as the river returns to its normal level

Lag time occurs because most rainwater enters rivers indirectly (e.g. surface runoff or infiltration).

Factors Affecting Flood Risk

PHYSICAL FACTORS

Relief

Steeper valley sides → water flows into channel faster → discharge increases more rapidly

Geology

Clay soils and some rocks are impermeable, increasing runoff.

Heavy rainfall

Water arrives too quickly to infiltrate. Lots of surface runoff increases discharge.

AND/OR

Prolonged rainfall

Saturates the soil so further rainfall can't infiltrate, increasing runoff into rivers.

HUMAN FACTORS

Land use

Impermeable building materials / surfaces (e.g. concrete / tarmac) increase surface runoff. Drains rapidly transport runoff to rivers, increasing discharge.

Trees intercept and store rainwater → cutting them down increases the amount of water entering river channels.

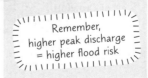

Remember, higher peak discharge = higher flood risk

Flooding and Flood Management

Management Strategies for Flooding

HARD ENGINEERING — structures built to control the flow of rivers and reduce flooding.

Method	Benefits	Disadvantages
Dams and reservoirs	Control water flow. Potential for hydroelectric power.	Dams are expensive. Construction can flood settlements.
Channel straightening	Water leaves area faster → less build up.	Flooding may happen downstream. Fast-moving water causes erosion.
Embankments	River capacity increased.	Expensive. Can overflow / break.
Flood relief channels	Control over diverted water.	Increased discharge where relief channel rejoins the river.

SOFT ENGINEERING — schemes set up using knowledge of a river and its processes.

Method	Benefits	Disadvantages
Flood warnings & preparation	Give people time to move possessions / evacuate.	Not preventative. Building modification is expensive. False sense of security.
Flood plain zoning	Fewer impermeable surfaces reduces flood risk and impacts.	Urban expansion limited. Can't help existing settlements.
Planting trees	Less discharge and soil erosion.	Less farmland available.
River restoration	Lower discharge. Requires little maintenance. Better habitats.	Local flood risk can increase.

Flood Management Scheme — Oxford

 2007 floods → 250 homes evacuated.

 EXAMPLE

Scheme will protect city centre, divert water from densely populated areas and involve:
• increased water storage • bypass channel • planting trees • flood walls

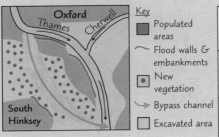

Key
■ Populated areas
~ Flood walls & embankments
⊡ New vegetation
⇢ Bypass channel
▢ Excavated area

	Issues	Benefits
Social	Forced land sales. Noisy construction.	Footpaths improved. Residents feel more secure.
Econ.	Expensive (£120m).	1000+ buildings protected. Cheaper insurance.
Environ.	2000 trees felled.	New riverside habitats.

Glacial Processes

Erosion and Weathering

Glaciers move downhill due to the weight of ice.

BASAL SLIDING — the movement of glaciers using meltwater under ice as lubricant.

Glaciers erode the landscape in two ways:

> ABRASION — rock stuck in the ice grinds against rock below the glacier.
>
> PLUCKING — meltwater at base / back / sides of glacier freezes onto rock. Glacier moves forward → pieces of rock pulled out.

I prefer the thaw part of weathering.

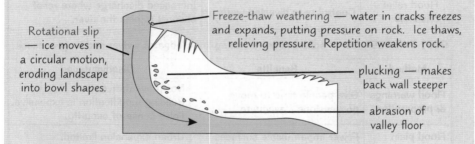

Rotational slip — ice moves in a circular motion, eroding landscape into bowl shapes.

Freeze-thaw weathering — water in cracks freezes and expands, putting pressure on rock. Ice thaws, relieving pressure. Repetition weakens rock.

plucking — makes back wall steeper

abrasion of valley floor

Transportation & Deposition

TILL — mixture of material (e.g. sand, clay, rocks) carried by glaciers.

Glaciers can transport material over large distances. Material can be:

- frozen into glacier
- carried on glacier's surface
- pushed ahead (bulldozing)

Material deposited on valley floor when:

- the glacier is overloaded
- the ice melts

Fine material (e.g. sand, gravel) washed away from front of glacier by meltwater streams. Streams sort material by size and deposit it in layers called outwash.

Historical Ice Coverage — UK

Many glacial periods in last 2.6m years. Last glacial period about 20 000 yrs ago. Ice has shaped the UK landscape.

☐ Max. extent of ice in last glacial period

Scotland

Leeds

Ireland

Wales

London

Bristol Channel

29

Glacial Landforms

Landforms of Glacial Erosion

Arête — narrow, steep-sided ridge formed when two glaciers flow in parallel valleys.

Corrie — steep-sided armchair shape with a lip at the bottom end. Formed by rotational slip.

Ribbon lake — long thin lake formed where soft rock is eroded more than surrounding hard rock.

Glacial trough — steep-sided valley with flat floor. Formed when glacier erodes V-shaped valley into U-shape.

Pyramidal peak — pointed peak, ≥ 3 sides. Formed by back-to-back glaciers.

Truncated spur — cliff-like edges on valley side. Formed when ridges are cut off as glacier moves past.

Hanging valley — valley formed by small tributary glacier.

Landforms of Glacial Deposition

DRUMLINS — elongated hills.
Upstream → round, blunt, steep.
Downstream → pointed, gentle slope.

ice flow — side view — aerial view

ERRATICS — rocks moved to an area with a different rock type.

MORAINES — a landform made of deposited till.
Four types: Lateral — eroded from valley walls, carried on ice at sides of glacier.

Medial — glaciers collide, two lateral moraines join.

Ground — material from base of glacier.

Terminal — abraded or plucked material at front of glacier, deposited as semicircular mounds.

Glacial Landforms — Snowdonia

Glacial landscape in north Wales, e.g. the Glyders.

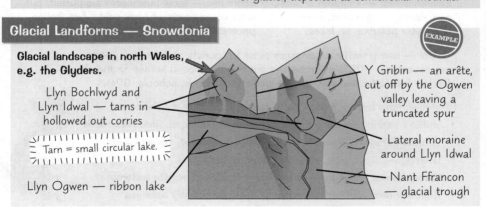

Llyn Bochlwyd and Llyn Idwal — tarns in hollowed out corries

Tarn = small circular lake.

Llyn Ogwen — ribbon lake

Y Gribin — an arête, cut off by the Ogwen valley leaving a truncated spur

Lateral moraine around Llyn Idwal

Nant Ffrancon — glacial trough

Land Use in Glacial Landscapes

Economic Uses of Glaciated Areas

 Forestry — coniferous forests grown in upland areas, used for building materials, paper and furniture.

 Quarrying — for slate, granite and limestone.

 Tourism — landscapes and outdoor activities attract tourists.

 Farming — sheep farming common in upland areas, crops grown on valley floor.

The people involved in these land uses can come into conflict — tourists can disrupt farming (e.g. scaring sheep) so farmers may try to block footpaths.

Development and Conservation — Conflicts

Development provides employment, roads and facilities. Conservationists want to preserve the environment.

Developers think...	Conservationists think...
Tourism and farming provide jobs and contribute to the UK economy.	Farming can damage the environment. Plantations don't support as many species as mixed forests.
Glacial areas can provide renewable energy (e.g. hydroelectric power).	Developments and construction sites destroy habitats and deter tourists. Logging damages habitats.
Developing roads / infrastructure for tourists can benefit local people too.	Tourist infrastructure may be unnecessary — people visit glacial areas for their natural appeal.

Tourism — The Lake District

EXAMPLE

The Lake District National Park attracts almost 19.2m tourists every year → lots of scenery, cultural sites and outdoor activities. Tourism has big impacts:

Environmental — footpath erosion, cars damage vegetation, noise and water pollution on lakes.

Economic — local businesses supported, but work often seasonal / low paid. Avg. house price £350 000+ → locals priced out.

Social — heavy traffic, businesses cater to tourists → everyday goods are expensive, ~25% of properties are holiday/second homes → there's limited / underfunded services for locals (e.g. buses, schools, GPs).

Strategies have been put in place to tackle impacts of tourism:
- Traffic / parking — using public transport encouraged, improved roads
- Footpath erosion — resurfacing, signposts, fencing, reseeding
- Littering — signs, bins, volunteer litter-pickers
- Water / noise pollution — speed limits, limited zones for watersports
- House prices — affordable housing, local occupancy schemes

Urban Growth

Urbanisation is Happening Fastest in Poorer Countries

URBANISATION — growth in proportion of people living in urban areas.

	Urbanisation Rate	Approx. % in urban areas
HICs	Low, less than 1%	80%
LICs	High, up to 6%	30%
NEEs	Around 2%	50%

Urbanisation has already happened in HICs.

~55% world population lives in urban areas

Causes of Urbanisation

RURAL-URBAN MIGRATION — movement from countryside to cities.

Push Factors (from rural areas)	Pull Factors (to urban areas)
Slower recovery from natural disasters.	More jobs and better pay.
Mechanisation → fewer farm jobs.	Better healthcare / education.
Desertification → land unproductive.	Family already there.
Unstable income (harvest dependent).	Hope for better quality of life.

Young migrate for work → have children.
Better urban healthcare → life expectancy increases.

leads to → NATURAL INCREASE — birth rate > death rate = population growth.

High urbanisation rates → MEGACITIES — urban area with 10 million+ residents. ← E.g. Mumbai, India.

Lagos, Nigeria (an NEE) — Rapid Urban Growth

CASE STUDY

Regionally Important:

Migrant population = cultural diversity.

Well connected → important for trade.

Benin | Niger
NIGERIA
Lagos
Cameroon

Population over 14 million.
Fast annual growth rate of 3.2% because:

Independence from Colonial Rule in 1960:

Economic development — resources (e.g. oil) no longer British controlled.

Gov. financed construction → jobs.

Natural Increase: Birth rate > death rate.

Nationally Important:

80% of Nigeria's industry.

Capital city until 1991.

Rural-Urban Migration:

Escape poverty.

Flee conflict in neighbouring countries.

Nigeria's birthrate = 35.2 per 1000 people. World average = 19.

Internationally Important:

West African financial centre.

5th largest African economy.

Port / airport → global trade.

Ex-slaves & descendants returned from 1800s on.

Urban Growth — Lagos

Urban Growth in Lagos Compared To Rural Nigeria

SOCIAL:
- 💊 More hospitals and medicines.
- ✏️ Almost 20 000 schools.
- ⚡ Better access to electricity.
- 💧 Safe, piped-in water.

ECONOMIC:
- 💰 Incomes up to 4x higher.
- 🏗️ Lots of construction jobs.
- 🐟 Government depts, manufacturing, fishing.
- 🎬 Music and 'Nollywood' film industry.

Five Challenges of Rapid Growth

> 66% of people in Lagos live in slums.

1 SLUMS & SQUATTER SETTLEMENTS

- Housing demand > supply → house prices rise → illegal settlements (slums).
- Housing = flimsy wooden huts → demolished to clean up city → evictions.

2 LITTLE ACCESS TO CLEAN WATER, SANITATION AND ENERGY

- Water demand > supply → prices inflated by informal sellers.
- Toilet waste contaminates water sources → disease, e.g. cholera.
- Neighbourhoods take turns to receive electricity. Some illegal connections.

3 INSUFFICIENT SERVICES

Many families can't afford school / healthcare. Not enough facilities.

4 UNEMPLOYMENT & CRIME

Too few formal jobs → alternatives, e.g. scavenging / gangs.

> Informal jobs have no legal protection → stalls may be bulldozed for new developments.

5 ENVIRONMENTAL ISSUES

- Only 40% of waste collected. Dumps contain toxic waste.
- Unregulated factory waste disposal → water pollution.
- Severe traffic congestion → air pollution.

Urban Planning to Improve Quality of Life — Makoko

EXAMPLE

The Makoko Floating School prototype was built in 2013:

SOCIAL BENEFITS
- Free education.
- Built by locals — gained skills.
- Community spirit.

ECONOMIC BENEFITS
- Improved job prospects.
- School success → gov. launch plan to regenerate slum with homes and biogas plant.

ENVIRONMENTAL BENEFITS
- Sustainable — used local materials, solar power and rainwater.
- Floats — flood safe.

Sadly, the school collapsed after a storm in 2016.

UK Cities

UK Cities — Distribution

The UK population distribution is very uneven.

Lowland areas — **easy to build on, milder climate.**

Coastal — **for harbours and ports.**

Near mineral deposits **(e.g. coal) — industrial development.**

CONURBATIONS — urban areas formed by towns merging.

Liverpool — a Port City in North West England

CASE STUDY

On the River Mersey estuary → **export of goods / culture.**

Internationally significant — **UNESCO World Heritage Site,** many foreign tourists → **major contribution to economy.**

Nationally significant — **3000 manufacturing companies** → **50 000+ jobs.**

It's also the World Capital City of Pop, and a European Capital of Culture.

1 in 8 Liverpudlians have an ethnic minority background.

Migration has influenced Liverpool's character:

1 National Migration

Late 1700s / Early 1800s: Welsh migrants → **industry / canals / railways.**

1845: Irish migrants due to famine.

2 International Migration

Port built in 1715.

Europe's first Chinatown.

UK's oldest Black African community.

Urban Change in Liverpool — Opportunities

CASE STUDY

Port and manufacturing centre ⟹ Tourist destination and creative industries centre

ENVIRONMENTAL:

Urban greening
Developing and preserving open spaces.
E.g. Liverpool ONE shopping and leisure complex includes a five-acre park.

Cycle / pedestrian routes
Reduced greenhouse gases.

Some traditional industry remains, e.g. car manufacturing at Halewood, and Liverpool2 (container port, opened 2016).

SOCIAL AND ECONOMIC:

Cultural mixing
Diversity in foods, festivals, etc.

Recreation / entertainment
E.g. Echo Arena sport / concert venue — on brownfield site (disused land) at Kings Dock.

Employment
160 000 tourism / service jobs.

'Baltic Triangle' area: old factories / warehouses → creative industries.

Integrated transport systems
Merseytravel operates city's bus, train and ferry networks — easy to get around.

UK Cities

Urban Change in Liverpool — Challenges

ENVIRONMENTAL:

Dereliction

Wealthy left → buildings abandoned and vandalised, e.g. Toxteth.

Using brownfield / greenfield sites

Suburbs grow → construction on greenfield sites → habitats destroyed.

Brownfield sites — better for environment but need decontamination.

Waste disposal

Population grows → more waste, less storage space.

SOCIAL AND ECONOMIC:

Urban deprivation

Industrial decline → inner city v. deprived.

Housing inequality

Regeneration increased inequality — replacement housing unaffordable to many.

Education and employment inequality

Deprived areas → low incomes, high unemployment.

Anfield youth unemployment = 8.5%, UK avg. = 2.8%.

Unhealthy lifestyles

Drinking, smoking and poor diets common in deprived areas → lower life expectancies.

Urban Sprawl — Pressure on Rural-Urban Fringe

Liverpool sprawled → Merseyside conurbation created.

Effects on rural-urban fringe:

Housing on greenfield land → open spaces / ecosystems lost.

Out-of-town developments, e.g. Knowsley Business Park, on cheaper land → rural land lost, pollution, congestion.

Commuter settlements formed → challenges:

House prices rise — locals can't afford to stay.

Businesses suffer — people aren't around much.

Pollution, congestion and parking problems increase.

URBAN SPRAWL — unplanned growth of urban areas into countryside.

RURAL-URBAN FRINGE — where urban and rural land uses mix.

COMMUTER SETTLEMENTS — places where most residents work elsewhere.

The Anfield Project — Urban Regeneration

Anfield was v. deprived — derelict housing, high crime.

£260 million regeneration project:

REGENERATION — redevelopment of urban area to improve quality of life.

SOCIAL AND ECONOMIC FEATURES:

>£36m spent refurbishing derelict housing.

Sports and Community Centre refurbished, new health centre and school.

New high street planned — existing and local businesses encouraged to move in.

ENVIRONMENTAL FEATURES:

£4.5m scheme to create tree-lined, wider pavements and a pedestrian-friendly area.

Stanley Park — dead trees replaced, footpath improved.

Sustainable Urban Living

Water & Energy Conservation Schemes

WATER CONSERVATION

Take only as much as is naturally replaced.

Schemes reduce usage by:

- collecting rainwater for gardens
- efficient toilets
- water meters

Curitiba, Brazil, cut water use with hosepipe bans and having separate non-drinking water systems.

Curitiba also has dedicated bus lanes for biodiesel buses.

ENERGY CONSERVATION

Burning fossil fuels is unsustainable:

- they'll run out.
- they release greenhouse gases.

Use of fossil fuels reduced by:

- Promoting renewables — letting homeowners sell excess electricity from solar panels.
- Efficiency rules for new homes.
- Promoting public transport use.

Green Space Creation

Green spaces...

- provide cooler areas away from bustle to relax in → happiness.
- encourage exercise / cycling → health benefits.
- reduce air pollution.
- reduce runoff → less flooding.

Curitiba landowners who created parks were tax exempt.

Waste Recycling

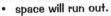
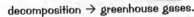

Landfill is unsustainable:

- space will run out.
- decomposition → greenhouse gases.

Recycling → saves resources, less landfill.
Schemes include:

- Kerbside collections.
- Large item recycling.
- Websites, e.g. Freecycle™.

In Curitiba, food / bus tickets are exchanged for recycling.

Traffic Congestion Causes Problems

 environmental: pollution / greenhouse gases.

 economic: e.g. delivery delays.

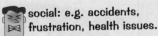 social: e.g. accidents, frustration, health issues.

Congestion can be reduced by:

Urban transport strategies which encourage public transport use, e.g.

- London Underground — 3m daily users.
- Electronic 'Oyster' cards increase convenience of London transport.
- Self-service bike hire in cities.

Managing traffic flow, e.g.

- Ring roads and pedestrianised areas.
- Congestion charges.
- Bus lanes — bus faster than driving.
- Parking restrictions help traffic flow, e.g. 'urban clearways'.

Measuring Development

Measures of Development

DEVELOPMENT — a country's progress in economic growth, use of technology and improving welfare.

GLOBAL DEVELOPMENT GAP — difference in development between more and less developed countries.

Measure	What it is	⬆/⬇ = increases/decreases with development
Gross National Income (GNI) per head (in US$)	Total value of goods and services produced in a year (inc. overseas income) divided by the population.	⬆
Birth rate	Live births per thousand per year.	⬇
Death rate	Deaths per thousand per year.	⬇
Infant mortality rate	No. of babies who die before 1 year old, per thousand born.	⬇
People per doctor	Avg. no. people for each doctor.	⬇
Literacy rate	% adults who can read and write.	⬆
Access to safe water	% with clean drinking water.	⬆
Life expectancy	Average age lived to.	⬆

Limitations of measures:

- Variations within a country not shown.

  Qatar's GNI per person is high — few extremely rich but many poor.

- Single indicators may be misleading.

  Cuba has low birth rate but fairly high death rate.

Classification by Wealth

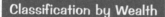

LOWER INCOME COUNTRIES (LICs) — Poorest, very low GNI per head. E.g. Somalia and Afghanistan.

HIGHER INCOME COUNTRIES (HICs) — Wealthiest, high GNI per head. E.g. UK, USA, Canada, France.

NEWLY EMERGING ECONOMIES (NEEs) — rapidly getting richer, moving from primary to secondary industry. E.g. the BRICS and MINT countries.

BRICS = Brazil, Russia, India, China and South Africa. MINT = Mexico, Indonesia, Nigeria and Turkey.

Measuring Development

The Human Development Index (HDI)

- Combines GNI per head, life expectancy and education level.
- Tells you about a country's economic development and quality of life
- Values between 0 and 1. 1 = most developed
- Country classifications similar to GNI per head.

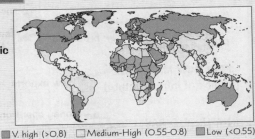

■ V. high (>0.8) ☐ Medium-High (0.55-0.8) ■ Low (<0.55)

Demographic Transition Model (DTM)

Shows how birth rates and death rates affect population growth.

Birth rate > death rate ➡ population grows — natural increase

Death rate > birth rate ➡ population shrinks — natural decrease

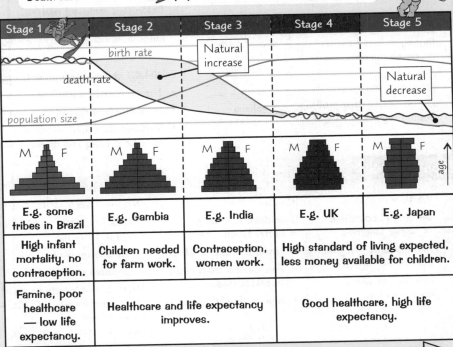

Stage 1	Stage 2	Stage 3	Stage 4	Stage 5
E.g. some tribes in Brazil	E.g. Gambia	E.g. India	E.g. UK	E.g. Japan
High infant mortality, no contraception.	Children needed for farm work.	Contraception, women work.	High standard of living expected, less money available for children.	
Famine, poor healthcare — low life expectancy.	Healthcare and life expectancy improves.		Good healthcare, high life expectancy.	

DEVELOPMENT

Uneven Development

Physical Causes

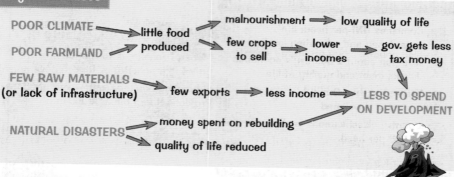

POOR CLIMATE ———→ little food produced

POOR FARMLAND ——↗

→ malnourishment ⟹ low quality of life

↘ few crops to sell ⟹ lower incomes ⟹ gov. gets less tax money

FEW RAW MATERIALS
(or lack of infrastructure) ——→ few exports ⟹ less income ⟹ LESS TO SPEND ON DEVELOPMENT

NATURAL DISASTERS ——→ money spent on rebuilding ↗

↘ quality of life reduced

Economic Causes

POOR TRADE LINKS —
Less trading = less income
to spend on development.

DEBT — Paying back
money = less to spend
on development.

PRIMARY-PRODUCT
ECONOMY — Low profits,
fluctuating prices.

In 2018, the price of cocoa dropped below the cost of production in Ghana.

Historical Causes

COLONISED countries held back.
- Industry development prevented.
- Colonisers removed raw materials, sold back manufactured goods.

CONFLICT slows development.
- Money spent on warfare.
- Infrastructure damaged.
- Services disrupted — affects infant mortality and literacy rates.

Consequences

WEALTH

Developed countries
= higher incomes.

More wealth = higher
standard of living.

Inequalities within
countries too.

In 2017, Kenya's richest 10% earned 23 times more than the poorest 10%.

HEALTH

Developed countries
= better healthcare.
- Lower infant mortality.
- Few deaths from easily treatable diseases.
- Higher life expectancy.

UK life expectancy is 81, but Chad's is 53.

INTERNATIONAL MIGRATION

People from LICs and NEEs
move to HICs to:
- escape conflict
- improve quality of life.

Migrants contribute to HICs'
economies instead of LICs' —
development
gap increases.

Reducing the Global Development Gap

Seven Strategies to Reduce the Gap

1 FOREIGN-DIRECT INVESTMENT (FDI)

Foreign countries buy property / invest.
- Access to finance / expertise.
- Improved infrastructure / services.

2 AID

South Sudan improved access to water, healthcare and education using UK aid in 2018-2019.

Money / resources for development provided by charity or foreign government.

Aid money could be lost — corruption.
Projects stop if money runs out.

3 FAIR TRADE

Farmers get a fair price for goods.
- Fair Trade label shows standards met.
- Buyers pay extra → help LIC's develop.
- Retailers may keep some extra profits.

4 INTERMEDIATE TECHNOLOGY

Tools, machines and systems that improve quality of life but are simple and affordable to buy / maintain.

5 MICROFINANCE LOANS

Small loans, e.g. for starting business / buying livestock.
Can encourage debt.

6 INDUSTRIAL DEVELOPMENT

Productivity, skills and infrastructure improved → boosts GNI and development.

7 DEBT RELIEF

Zambia had $4 billion of debt cancelled in 2005 — allowed them to start a free healthcare scheme.

Cancelling debt or lowering interest rates.
Give LICs more to spend on development.

Tourism and Development — Kenya

Kenya's culture, wildlife, climate and scenery attracts tourists.

EXAMPLE

- Lower income country in East Africa.
- Government boosted tourism to increase development by reducing visiting costs.
- Visa fees cut and charter airline landing fees dropped →
  No. of tourists increased from 0.9 million in 1995 to 1.4 million in 2017.

BENEFITS

Tourism = nearly 4% of GDP — improves development / quality of life.

Tourism employs >1.1 million people.

Investment in transport infrastructure benefits locals and boosts tourism.

National park entry fees used to protect environment and wildlife.

NEGATIVES

Money often goes to HIC companies — doesn't close development gap.

Maasai communities forced off land to create game reserves.

Vehicles destroy vegetation / disturb animals.

Tourist numbers fluctuate — unreliable source of jobs and income.

CASE STUDY: Economic Development in India

A Rapidly Developing NEE

World's second largest pop. and still growing.

- Regionally important → trade links with SE Asia and Middle East.
- Globally important → exports services and manufactured goods, member of World Trade Organisation and G20.

Social

HDI = 0.64 — large inequalities / poverty.
Literacy rate < 75% — but improving.

Political

Former British colony — now democratic.

Environmental

Varied landscape — Himalayas, Thar Desert.
Floodplains (Ganges and Indus) → fertile land.
Long coastline — attracts tourists.

Cultural

Over 22 official languages.
Religions include Hinduism and Islam.
'Bollywood' films / Bhangra dancing.

Changing Industrial Structure

GDP measures wealth.

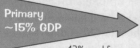

Primary ~15% GDP — 42% workforce

Secondary ~28% GDP — 24% workforce

Tertiary & quaternary 62% GDP — 34% workforce

Primary	Agriculture
Secondary	Manufacturing
Tertiary	Services (e.g. call centres)
Quaternary	Knowledge (e.g. IT)

Manufacturing industry:
- Stimulates economic development.
- Provides reliable jobs (unlike seasonal agricultural work).

Industry attracted → Workers spend income → Businesses pay taxes → Gov. spends on development

Transnational Corporations (TNCs)

TNCs build factories in LICs → cheap labour, fewer regulations = more profit.
TNC offices / HQs usually in HICs → more people with administrative skills.

Advantages for host

- Employment
- TNCs pay taxes.
- May run development programs.

Unilever employs >16 000 in India.

Disadvantages for host

- Job losses if factories close / relocate.
- Possible environmental problems.
- Pay and conditions may be poor.
- Some profits leave India.

Unilever's Project Shakti provides loans and saleable products to help poor women become entrepreneurs.

Unilever is Dutch-British → profits may leave India.

Economic Development in India

CASE STUDY

Changing Relationships with the Wider World

POLITICAL RELATIONSHIPS

- Tension with Pakistan and China over land ownership.
- Relationships built with other nations, e.g. the Act East policy increases India's influence and regional security.
- TAPI pipeline — will carry natural gas from Turkmenistan to India (through Afghanistan and Pakistan).

TRADING RELATIONSHIPS

- Government reduced trade barriers, e.g. import taxes.
- Free trade agreements.
- TNCs operating in India increase trade and FDI.

E.g. Asia-Pacific Trade Agreement with Bangladesh, China, S. Korea and Sri Lanka.

Aid Received

Type	How it works	Impacts	Example
SHORT-TERM	Money / supplies for emergencies.	Helps survival — not recovery.	UNICEF provided supplies after flooding in N. India.
LONG-TERM	Investment in development projects.	Can improve education / infrastructure etc. Can be misused, e.g. by corrupt officials.	Until 2015, the UK sent £200m per year for education, healthcare & sanitation improvements.
TOP-DOWN	An organisation / government decides how to use aid.	Can improve economy, but may not help poorest, or be supported by locals.	The Sardar Sarovar dam provides water / HEP, but displaced >300k people.
BOTTOM-UP	Given directly to locals → they decide how to use it.	Improves health, skills and income in poor communities.	Women trained to repair pumps in Gujarat → skills / improved water supply.

Impacts on Quality of Life

More jobs, increases in wages. ➡ More money to improve life, e.g. clean water supply.

HDI has increased from 0.49 in 2000 to 0.64.

Some jobs have poor working conditions — reduced quality of life.

Impacts on Environment

Delhi has world's worst air pollution.

Fossil fuels are most used, so:

Increasing energy consumption. ➡ More greenhouse gas emissions and pollution.

Resource demand can destroy habitats. ← Coal mining damaged Bengal tigers habitats.

But: people can afford to spend more on protecting the environment.

Unit 2B — The Changing Economic World

Economic Development in the UK

Moving Towards a Post-Industrial Economy

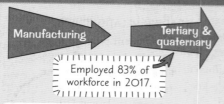

Manufacturing → Tertiary & quaternary

Employed 83% of workforce in 2017.

Important industries:
Services — e.g. retail (4 million jobs).
IT — 670 000+ jobs.
Finance — global HQs in UK.
R&D — £33bn spent in 2016.

SCIENCE & BUSINESS PARKS

Near universities — researchers.

Quaternary industries — develop technology.

Increasing demand for high-tech products.

Clustered together → boost each other.

City outskirts — near housing & transport links.

Three Main Causes of Economic Change

% of GDP from foreign trade increasing.

1 DE-INDUSTRIALISATION

Automation → job losses.
Cheaper goods from abroad.

2 GLOBALISATION

Manufacturing moved overseas — cheaper labour.
Some tertiary / quaternary operations moved to UK.

3 GOVERNMENT POLICIES

- 1980s — manufacturing industries privatised → jobs lost but efficiency increased.
- Deregulation (removing restrictions / taxes) → attracts investors to the UK.
- Trade agreements / WTO membership → easier to operate across the world.

World Trade Organisation

Impacts on Environment

- Pollutants / greenhouses gases released, high energy / water use.
- Modern industry more sustainable — increased energy and waste disposal costs, stricter regulations.

The Unicorn Group — manufacturer in Lisburn, NI.

 EXAMPLE

Increased sustainability — solar panels, 100% of electricity from renewable energy, biomass boilers, leftover materials recycled.

Transport Network

Congestion slows economic development.

- Road capacity — upgrades to smart motorways, e.g. M4.
- Rail infrastucture, e.g. proposed HS2 line — faster.
- Airport capacity — third runway at Heathrow → noise / pollution fears.
- Port capacity — London Gateway opened on Thames in 2013 — can handle largest container ships.

Economic Development in the UK

Links to Other Countries

Trade — £160bn overseas exports per year.

Culture — exported worldwide, e.g. Aardman Animations.
Immigration shaped diverse UK culture, e.g. food.

Transport — Channel Tunnel, airports = international hubs.

Electronic communications — telephones / internet.
Trans-Atlantic cables routed via UK.

The Commonwealth —
53 states, many former
UK colonies. Promotes
co-operation and trade
between members.

*The UK left the EU in 2020.
There's free movement of goods /
people between EU member states.*

Change in Rural Areas

AREA	South Lakeland, Cumbria	North Somerset
POPULATION CHANGE	Decrease	Increase
REASONS	Job losses — agriculture / manufacturing.	Easy access to Bristol.
ECONOMIC IMPACTS	Shop closures, job losses.	House price rise, more jobs, higher wages.
SOCIAL IMPACTS	Younger people moved away. Older population stayed.	Congestion, full schools, elderly people move in.

Elderly pop. = strained health / social care.

Regional Differences

NORTH-SOUTH DIVIDE:

Heavy industry decline —
worse impact on north.

Service industry growth —
mostly benefited south.

Economic / social
indicators (wages,
health, GCSEs) tend
to be better in south.

*Life expectancy for
men born 2012 in:
Glasgow = 72.6 years,
East Dorset = 82.9 years.*

Exceptions exist — i.e. wealthy areas in
north, areas of deprivation in south.

Three approaches to resolving regional differences:

1 DEVOLUTION OF POWERS

Allows countries / local councils
to use money how they think
best, e.g. improving public
transport, regeneration projects.

2 ENTERPRISE ZONES

~50 created across UK.

Companies get benefits for locating in zones:
• reduced taxes   • simpler planning rules
• good infrastructure, e.g. superfast broadband

*Sheffield City Region
Enterprise Zone has
created 16 000 jobs.*

3 THE NORTHERN POWERHOUSE

Gov. plan to attract investment and improve transport links in north.
Includes extending superfast broadband and improving schools.

But: often unclear how money will be spent. Only focuses on big cities.

Resources — Globally and in the UK

Vital Resources — Food, Water and Energy

FOOD —
Needed to avoid undernourishment (not getting enough food) and malnourishment (not getting the right balance of nutrients).
Malnourishment can limit children's development and increase disease risk.

WATER —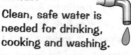
Clean, safe water is needed for drinking, cooking and washing.
Sanitation prevents the pollution of water sources by raw sewage, and water-borne diseases, e.g. cholera.
Needed to produce products such as food and clothes.

ENERGY —
Needed for industry, transport and home use.
Stable electricity supply = better quality of life.
No electricity → wood / kerosene used instead → deforestation / fumes.
Electricity can power pumps for wells to provide safe water.

Unequal Resource Distribution

Global supply and consumption is unequal. A country's consumption depends on:

1️⃣ RESOURCE AVAILABILITY — energy reserves, environment suited to food production.

2️⃣ WEALTH — to import resources, to produce resources using technology.

Country type	Consumption	Reason
HICs	High	Can afford resources. Higher standard of living.
NEEs	Increasing	Industry — population and wealth increasing.
LICs	Low	Can't afford to exploit or buy resources.

Water in the UK

Demand is rising — more appliances and larger population.

North and west ⟹ high rainfall = water surplus
South east and the Midlands ⟹ high population density = water deficit

Birmingham (deficit) is supplied with water from Wales (surplus).

Water quality can be affected by pollution, e.g. from fertilisers, vehicles, factories.
Strategies to manage water quality include:
- improving drainage systems.
- regulating fertiliser and pesticide use.

Water can be transferred from areas of surplus to areas of deficit, but:
- building dams and aqueducts is expensive.
- it affects wildlife.
- it can cause political issues.

Resources — Globally and in the UK

Food in the UK

Demand for certain types of food is growing:

Organic food production is strictly regulated.

High-value foods
Often grown in LICs, e.g. Ethiopia.
E.g. exotic fruits and vegetables, spices, coffee.

Seasonal products
Out-of-season foods imported all year round.
E.g. in winter, strawberries from Mexico.

Organic produce
Increased concerns about:
- how chemicals affect health.
- how food production affects environment.

BUT:
Imported food → More food miles → More CO_2 released → Larger carbon footprint + More environmental awareness → Demand for locally-sourced food increases

There is a growing trend towards agribusiness:
- large-scale industrial farms.
- more chemicals used, e.g. fertilisers.
- more machinery = fewer workers needed.

CARBON FOOTPRINT (of food) — the amount of greenhouse gas released while producing and transporting food.

Energy in the UK

In 2014, renewables generated 19% of UK electricity.

The energy mix has changed:
- decreased reliance on fossil fuels (coal, oil and gas).
- greater significance of renewables (wind, bioenergy, solar and hydroelectric power).

Aims to reduce CO_2 emissions → Decreased coal demand → Production drops

North Sea oil and gas being used up rapidly. → Extracting shale gas through fracking is being considered.

Exploiting energy resources can cause issues:

Economic issues	Environmental issues
Extracting fossil fuels is expensive — cost increases as reserves used up.	Burning fossil fuels releases CO_2 and other greenhouse gases.
Nuclear and renewable energy is more expensive for consumers.	Fracking may pollute groundwater and cause mini-earthquakes.
UK must import energy to meet demand.	Nuclear disasters and oil spills damage the environment.
Money needed for research into alternative sources.	Renewable energy generation damages ecosystems and may be an eyesore.

Food Supply and Demand

Global Patterns of Food Supply and Calorie Intake

Food production:

North America and East Asia ➡ High (surplus)

Central America and Africa ➡ Low (deficit)

Country type	Daily calorie intake
HICs	Higher — more food, more imports
LICs	Lower — less food, less imports
NEEs	Increasing — rising wealth

FOOD SECURITY — having access to enough nutritious food to stay healthy and active.

FOOD INSECURITY — NOT having access to enough food to stay healthy and active.

Two Reasons for Increase in Global Food Consumption

1 Rising population: **More people = more food needed.**

2 Economic development: • **Wealthier countries can buy and import more food.**
• Industrialised agriculture — food is cheaper.

Factors Affecting Food Supply

PHYSICAL

- Climate and extreme weather.
- Water stress — low rainfall or little water for irrigation.
- Pests and diseases reduce crop yields.

HUMAN

- Poverty — harder to own land, farm and import food.
- Technology — e.g. machinery makes farming more productive.
- Conflict — damaged farmland, unsafe trade routes, political relationships disrupted.

Impacts of Food Insecurity

FAMINE — widespread lack of food. Can lead to starvation and death.

UNDERNUTRITION — not eating enough nutrients to stay healthy.

Stunted growth affects ~40% of children under five in sub-Saharan Africa.

SOIL EROSION — over-cultivation and overgrazing damages farmland.

RISING FOOD PRICES — demand exceeds supply → higher prices → further insecurity.

SOCIAL UNREST — food shortages and high food prices can lead to looting, riots and civil wars.

Increasing Food Production

Five Strategies to Increase Food Supply

1 IRRIGATION

Artificially watering land in dry areas → better yields.

 Gravity flow — ditches and channels.

Sprinklers

Drip systems — small holes in pipes.

2 HYDROPONICS AND AEROPONICS

Growing plants without soil.
Expensive, but uses less water and
Lower disease / pest risk = less need for pesticides.

HYDROPONICS — plants grown in nutrient solution.

AEROPONICS — plants suspended in air.
Water containing nutrients sprayed onto roots.

3 BIOTECHNOLOGY

Involves genetically modified (GM) crops.
Increased yield, nutritional value, and resistance to pests, disease and drought.

But — environmental and ethical concerns, e.g. reduced biodiversity, disrupted ecosystems.

4 NEW GREEN REVOLUTION

Increases yields sustainably using:

• GM crops

• Traditional / organic methods, e.g. crop rotation, natural predators.

5 APPROPRIATE TECHNOLOGY

Methods suited to the local environment and people, e.g. their skills and wealth.

E.g. using an irrigation system constructed from local materials is more appropriate than an imported, high-tech system.

Burkina Faso — Large Scale Agricultural Development

EXAMPLE

Burkina Faso is an LIC in West Africa.

PROBLEMS:
Hot, dry, short rainy season → limited water.

Rising population → malnutrition, food insecurity.

RESPONSE:
Dams, reservoirs and canals built to provide reliable water supply for irrigation

The Bagrè Dam stores 1.7 billion m³ of water.

ADVANTAGES

• Reliable water supply from gravity-based irrigation systems.

• Paddy fields created — rice grown.

• More than 1500 jobs created.

• Dam is used for hydropower.

DISADVANTAGES

• Only irrigated 10% of planned area.

• Water loss — canals not maintained.

• Water too expensive for most farmers.

• People displaced and land lost.

• Opening dams can cause flooding.

Sustainable Food Supply

Low Impact Food Production

> Industrial agriculture uses 70% of world's fresh water supplies.

Type	What it involves
ORGANIC FARMING	• Natural processes **return nutrients to soil**. • Pesticides and animal supplements restricted → biodiversity protected. • Crops rotated, natural fertilisers → less environmental damage. • Sold near farm — fewer food miles.
PERMACULTURE	• Natural ecosystems recreated — protects wildlife and soil. • Mixed cropping — better use of space / light, fewer pests / diseases, less watering. • Natural predators → fewer pesticides needed.
URBAN FARMING INITIATIVES	• Farming in towns, e.g. allotments. • Local food — less food miles. • Cheaper — improves food security.
SUSTAINABLY SOURCED FISH AND MEAT	• Catch quotas — avoid overfishing. • Environmentally-friendly fishing methods. • Locally-sourced animal feed. • Eating all edible parts of animals. • Seaweed in cattle feed — decreased methane emissions.

> Urban farming reduces dependence on industrial agriculture.

Sustainable Consumption

Eat seasonal food, not imported food.

Reduced food miles

↓

Reduced carbon footprint

↓

Lower CO_2 emissions — these contribute to global warming

Waste less food.

Encouraged by schemes like 'Love Food Hate Waste'.

Supermarkets can help charities distribute waste food to those in need.

LIC Sustainability Scheme   (EXAMPLE)

• **Mali is a very dry LIC.**

• **Intensive farming → desertification → land less fertile.**

• **Farmers use AGROFORESTRY to grow maize between other plants:**

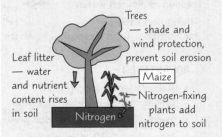

Trees — shade and wind protection, prevent soil erosion

Leaf litter — water and nutrient content rises in soil

Maize

Nitrogen-fixing plants add nitrogen to soil

Nitrogen

• **Maize yield increased.**

• **Soil protected → sustainable.**

Water Supply and Demand

Global Patterns of Water Security / Insecurity

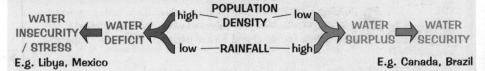

WATER INSECURITY / STRESS ← WATER DEFICIT ← high — POPULATION DENSITY — low → WATER SURPLUS → WATER SECURITY

low — RAINFALL — high

E.g. Libya, Mexico

E.g. Canada, Brazil

WATER STRESS — when demand exceeds supply or water is low quality.

WATER SECURITY — enough water to meet needs (e.g. personal, industrial, agricultural).

Global water demand is rising due to:

- Increasing population — more irrigation, drinking, cooking, etc.
- Economic development — increased manufacturing, energy production and living standards.

Factors Affecting Water Availability

PHYSICAL:

Climate
- Rainfall is needed to fill lakes and rivers.
- Higher temp → more water evaporates.

Geology

Rain runs off impermeable rock

Easy to get water from rivers and lakes.

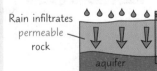

Rain infiltrates permeable rock

Hard to get water from underground stores.

aquifer

SOCIO-ECONOMIC:

Over-abstraction — water used > water replaced.

Pollution — e.g. by industry or animal waste.

Limited infrastructure — too few pipes / sewers.

Poverty — people can't afford water provider fees.

Water Insecurity Impacts

POLLUTION & DISEASE — using polluted water can lead to waterborne diseases, e.g. cholera.

REDUCED FOOD PRODUCTION — insufficient irrigation reduces crop growth, leading to starvation.

REDUCED INDUSTRIAL OUTPUT — less water = less manufacturing. Economy affected, incomes lowered.

CONFLICT — can occur when countries share a water source.

Actions of upstream countries affect countries downstream.

50

Increasing Water Supply

Four Ways to Increase Water Supply

1 Building a STORAGE DAM across a river traps water, creating a RESERVOIR. Water is released when there's a deficit.
But: floods farmland and forces people to relocate. Expensive.

2 WATER DIVERSION — a dam raises a river's water level and redirects water for irrigation or hydroelectric power.
No reservoir so less disruptive than a storage dam.

3 WATER TRANSFER SCHEMES — large-scale engineering projects that move water from areas of surplus to areas of deficit.
But: can cause wide-ranging problems (see below). Expensive.

4 DESALINATION removes salt from seawater either by evaporation and condensation, or by passing it through a membrane. Used by wealthy desert countries.
But: requires lots of energy. Expensive.

Desalination supplies 98.8% of Dubai's water.

South-North Water Transfer Project — China

EXAMPLE

Northern China — high population densities, expanding industry and increasing need for agricultural land = high demand for water.
Leads to WATER INSECURITY.

Government planned a South-North water project to transfer 44.8 billion m³ of water yearly:

- Cost $62 billion.
- Work began in 2002.
- Central and Eastern Routes completed by 2014.
- Western Route's completion planned for 2050.

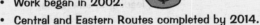

ADVANTAGES:
- Clean water for over 20 cities.
- Up to 100 million may benefit.
- Allows industrial development to continue in the north.
- Water provided for irrigation.
- Prevents over-abstraction, reducing land subsidence.

DISADVANTAGES:
- Flooding destroyed habitats.
- Construction harms ecosystems.
- More water stress / droughts in south.
- Farmland flooded, 345 000 people relocated with little compensation.
- Water supplied to Beijing is expensive and only available in urban areas.

Sustainable Water Supply

Sustainable Strategies to Increase Water Supply

Strategy	What it involves
WATER CONSERVATION	• Fix leaks in reservoirs, pipes and taps. • Use efficient toilets, washing machines, dishwashers, etc. • Irrigate to where water is needed. • Increase awareness of costs, e.g. fit water meters.
GROUNDWATER MANAGEMENT	• Monitor groundwater / pass laws to prevent over-abstraction. • Avoid fertilisers and fine companies that leak toxic waste. • Create international agreements to share groundwater sustainably.
RECYCLING	• Wastewater piped to treatment plants to make safe for reuse. • Most recycled water used for irrigation, industry, power plants and toilet flushing — but it can be treated further for drinking.
'GREY' WATER	• Water that is reused without treatment. • Mostly domestic wastewater (NOT from toilets — contaminated). • Clean enough for irrigation and flushing toilets, NOT for drinking. • Saves energy used in water treatment. • Systems expensive. Water must be used quickly (bacteria grow).

20% of water in the UK is lost to leaks.

Increasing Sustainable Water Supplies — Kenya

EXAMPLE

Kenya — hot, dry country in East Africa. Most rivers only flow during rainy season.

Rural communities can't store water — source may be 10 km away.

Solution: sand dams installed:

ADVANTAGES:

• Cheap to build, uses local materials, little maintenance.

• Height of dam can be raised each year to trap more sand and water.

• Water can be used for irrigation.

• Water is closer to community.

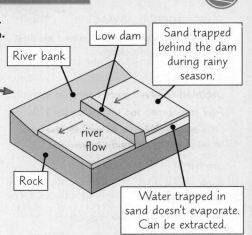

Low dam. Sand trapped behind the dam during rainy season. River bank. river flow. Rock. Water trapped in sand doesn't evaporate. Can be extracted.

Energy Supply and Demand

Energy Security

ENERGY SECURITY — having a reliable, uninterrupted and affordable supply of energy

ENERGY SURPLUS — having more energy than the population requires.

ENERGY DEFICIT — having less energy than the population requires.

A country's energy security depends on:

- available supplies
- population size
- average use per person

Global Patterns of Production and Consumption

Large reserves + ability to exploit $\implies$ high production, e.g. Iran, China, Russia

Few reserves / inability to exploit $\implies$ low production, e.g. Ireland, Sudan

Wealth $\rightarrow$ High standard of living $\rightarrow$ Use electricity, heating, devices $\rightarrow$ High energy consumption

Poverty $\rightarrow$ Low standard of living $\rightarrow$ Lifestyles less energy-dependent $\rightarrow$ Lower energy consumption

Factors Affecting Supply

PHYSICAL:

Amount of reserves and ease of extraction.

Suitability for renewables (climate / geology).

Likelihood of natural disasters.

TECHNOLOGICAL ADVANCES:

Possible / easier to exploit new / existing resources, e.g. fracking.

ECONOMIC:

Depleted reserves more costly to extract.

Fuel sometimes too expensive for LICs.

LICs may lack funds to exploit reserves or build energy infrastructure.

POLITICAL:

Political instability affects exports.

The Middle East's oil exports decreased during the Gulf War.

Stricter nuclear power regulations.

International CO_2 emission agreements.

Rising Energy Demand

RISING POPULATION — more people = more energy needed.

ECONOMIC DEVELOPMENT — more industry, more money = more energy-using goods bought.

TECHNOLOGICAL ADVANCES — new devices need energy.

Impacts of Energy Insecurity

 ENVIRONMENTAL DAMAGE — reserves in sensitive areas exploited.

 FOOD SHORTAGES — struggle to power farming equipment.

 INDUSTRIAL OUTPUT — reduced output → jobs lost, higher prices for consumers.

 CONFLICT — between areas of surplus and areas of deficit.

Increasing Energy Supplies

Renewable Energy Sources

Energy Type	Overview	Example
SOLAR	Water heaters are cheap. Photovoltaic cells are expensive — but excess energy can be sold. Unreliable — not always sunny.	Noor Complex, Morocco. Supplies 1m people.
HYDRO (HEP)	Dammed water falls and turns turbines. Adjustable output. Expensive. Habitat loss.	The Three Gorges Dam, China.
GEOTHERMAL	Water pumped underground → steam. Steam turns turbines or heats houses. Cheap, reliable, best in tectonically active areas.	Supplies 87% of Iceland's home heating and hot water.
TIDAL	Currents / water level changes turn turbines. Reliable. Expensive, variable output.	Proposed Swansea Bay Tidal Lagoon.
WAVE	Waves turn turbines. Expensive.	Being tested in Wales.
WIND	No greenhouse gas emissions once built. Unreliable.	2017: Denmark ran on wind power for a day.
BIOMASS	Plants / animal waste → burnt / make biofuel. Little technology needed — good for LICs. Renewable if sustainably managed.	USA produced 1m barrels of biofuel a day in 2015.

Non-Renewable Sources

FOSSIL FUELS

Reserves run out / become too hard to extract. BUT:

- New reserves may be found.
- Technology allows extraction of previously inaccessible reserves.

NUCLEAR POWER

Uranium will run out, but:

- New technology increases efficiency.
- New breeder reactors generate more fuel.

Fracking

FRACKING — liquid pumped into shale rock at high pressure, rock cracks to release trapped gas.

PROS:

Huge UK reserves — increases energy security.

Less polluting than other fossil fuels.

Cheaper than some renewables.

CONS:

Not sustainable — high water use, gas is non-renewable, burning it releases CO_2.

May pollute water and air.

May cause small earthquakes.

May slow down investment in renewable energy.

Fracking near Blackpool halted in 2019 due to safety concerns.

BAN FRACKING NOW

Don't pollute my water!

Sustainable Energy

Sustainable Energy and Carbon Footprints

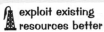

SUSTAINABLE ENERGY — provide energy today without preventing future generations from meeting energy needs.

Important because:
• Energy demand increasing with population.
• Non-renewable resources running out.

Humans must: 🔥 exploit existing resources better   〰️ find new renewable sources   ⚙️ use energy efficiently

CARBON FOOTPRINT — amount of greenhouse gases a person's activities produce. Includes direct and indirect emissions.

Direct emissions — from things that use energy, e.g. air travel.
Indirect emissions — from making things we buy, e.g. clothing.

Energy Conservation

Sustainable Design
• Insulate buildings.
• Fit efficient boilers and solar panels.
• Use electric vehicles.
• Use biofuel-powered vehicles.

Demand Reduction
• Incentives to reduce energy use — e.g. tax relief, congestion charges.
• Public transport improvements.
• Smart meters → awareness of use.

Use Technology to Increase Efficiency
• Energy saving light bulbs.
• Hybrid vehicles.
• Regenerative braking — storing energy lost when braking.
• Make engines more efficient.
• Combined Cycle Gas Turbine technology in power stations — lost heat recovered and used to generate more electricity.

I've been powered by coffee-bean biofuel since 2017.

Renewable Energy in Bihar, India (an NEE)

EXAMPLE

Unreliable electricity supply — 85% of people not connected to grid.
In 2007, local biomass used to supply electricity:

• Local rice husks used — a waste product.
• Small, local power plants — simple design.
• Electricity supplied to homes in 1.5 km range.

This scheme was very efficient — the rice husks and electricity don't travel far.

• By 2015, 84 rice husk power plants in Bihar → electricity for 200 000 people.
• Less need for diesel generators / kerosene lamps → reduced fossil fuel use.
• Local people trained → creates jobs and more sustainable.

Fieldwork

Data Collection

PRIMARY DATA — collected by yourself.

SECONDARY DATA — collected by someone else.

You start with a research question / hypothesis — you need to know the theory behind it.

Make sure you can justify your data collection method.

E.g. collecting the views of people in different age groups about a local issue.

Three sampling techniques:

1. **Random** — samples chosen at random.
2. **Systematic** — samples taken at regular intervals.
3. **Stratified** — samples taken from different groups to get good overall representation.

Data Presentation and Analysis

Describe your Data:

- Spot patterns / correlations / anomalies.
- Compare data sets.

Use statistical techniques, maps and graphs to help.

You might be asked how effective your presentation methods were.

Explain the Results:

- Explain why patterns exist.
- Use geographical knowledge and terms.

Conclusion

Summarise what the results show.

Answer the original question.

Explain:

- the answer.
- the evidence for the answer.
- how the results could be used further / fit into the wider geographical world.

Evaluation

Assess what you did — comment on:

Data collection methods:
- size of data sets.
- bias (unfairness).

Identify any problems with your methods.

Data limitations:
- Did it answer the question?
- Any other useful data?

Accuracy of results:
- Any errors?

ACCURATE RESULTS — very near true answer, few errors.

RELIABLE RESULTS — can be reproduced.

Validity of conclusion:
- Depends on reliability / accuracy of results.

VALID RESULTS — reliable and answer original question.

Maps

Three Rules For Describing Distributions

1. Describe the pattern and anomalies.

2. Make one point for each mark available.

3. Use place names / figures given.

If asked to explain distribution, describe it first.

Describing Locations

- Say where it is.
- Say what it's near.
- Use compass points.
- Use key words, e.g. use 'coast' instead of 'edge'.

Latitude and Longitude — Global Coordinates

LATITUDE LINES — Horizontal lines measuring distance north or south of the equator.

LONGITUDE LINES — Vertical lines measuring distance east or west of the Prime Meridian.

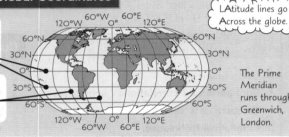

LAtitude lines go Across the globe.

The Prime Meridian runs through Greenwich, London.

Dot Maps

Identical dots show number and distribution.

Location of factories

• = 10 factories

Proportional Symbol Maps

Larger symbols = larger amounts

Car Parks in Drumshire

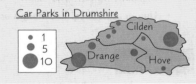

- • 1
- ● 5
- ● 10

Isolines

Isolines link places where something is the same.

E.g. Contours = same altitude. Isobars = same pressure.

Reading Isoline Maps:
- **On a line → read off value.**
- **Between two lines → estimate.**

Completing Isoline Maps:
- **Join dots with the same numbers.**
- **Never cross other isolines.**

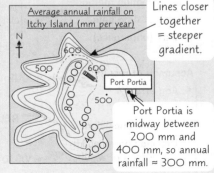

Average annual rainfall on Itchy Island (mm per year)

Lines closer together = steeper gradient.

Port Portia

Port Portia is midway between 200 mm and 400 mm, so annual rainfall ≈ 300 mm.

Maps

Choropleth Maps

Show variation using colours or patterns.

Draw patterns carefully.

People per km²

▯ = 0 — 99

▯▯ = 100 — 199

▯▯▯ = 200+

Flow Lines

Arrows show movement.

Arrow widths can show proportions.
E.g. about twice as many people come to the UK from the USA than from the Middle East.

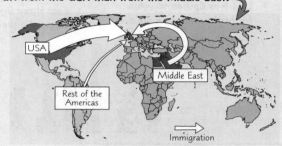

USA

Middle East

Rest of the Americas

Immigration

Desire Lines

- Show journeys between two places.
- Straight — don't follow roads.
- One line = one journey.

These are used to show how far people travelled to get to a place, e.g. a shop, and where they've come from.

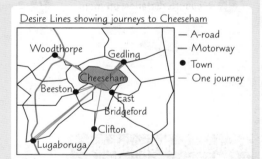

Desire Lines showing journeys to Cheeseham

Woodthorpe · Gedling · Beeston · Cheeseham · East Bridgeford · Clifton · Lugaboruga

— A-road
— Motorway
● Town
— One journey

Ordnance Survey (OS®) Symbols

━━ Motorway
━━ Main (A) road
━━ Secondary (B) road
⊰ Bridge
── Railway
–·– County boundary
National Park boundaries

▭ Building
⬤ Bus station
┄┄ Footpaths
⚡ Viewpoint
ℹ Tourist information centre
P Parking
+ ■ ● Places of worship

Compass Points

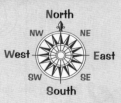

North
NW   NE
West — East
SW   SE
South

Remember: Never Eat Soggy Wheat.

Geographical Skills

Maps

Grid References

Across value = easting.
Up value = northing.

Four Figure:

- First two figures = value for left edge of square.
- Last two figures = value for bottom edge of square.

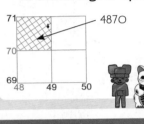

4870

Six Figure:

- Divide square into tenths across and up.
- First three figures = value for left edge of square and number of tenths across.
- Last three figures = value for bottom edge of square and number of tenths up.

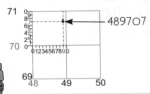

489707

Two Steps to Find a Distance

1 Measure distance on map.

2.2 cm

2 Compare distance to scale.

Scale 1:50 000
2 centimetres to 1 kilometre (one grid square)
Kilometres

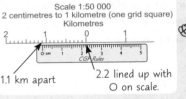

1.1 km apart

2.2 lined up with O on scale.

Contours and Spot Heights

Contour lines join points of equal altitude.

Height above sea level / altitude (m)

Lines close together = steeper slope

Spot height

Nick Nobble
• 532

Herman's Hump
• 558

530

540

520

Petey Pike
570

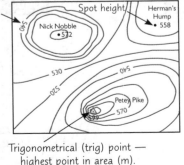

Trigonometrical (trig) point — highest point in area (m).

Sketching Maps

Use a pencil.

Copy the grid.

Get main shapes right.

Measure key points.

Add labels.

Check number of marks and time left to decide on level of detail.

Charts and Graphs

Bar Charts

① **To read bar charts:**

Find top of bar. ⟹ Go to scale. ⟹ Read number.

② **To read divided bar charts:**

Find top and bottom of relevant part of bar. ⟹ Read numbers off scale. ⟹ Subtract bottom value from top.

③ **To complete bar charts:**

Find number on vertical scale. ⟹ Trace line across to top of bar. ⟹ Use ruler to draw bar.

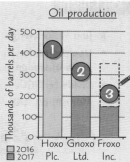

Oil production

Thousands of barrels per day

☐ 2016 ▨ 2017

Hoxo Plc.   Gnoxo Ltd.   Froxo Inc.

Histograms

Use histograms for data divided into intervals.

Draw and plot them like bar charts but remember to check bar widths.

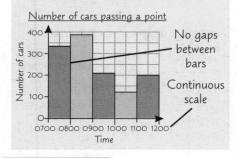

Number of cars passing a point

Number of cars

0700 0800 0900 1000 1100 1200
Time

No gaps between bars

Continuous scale

Line Graphs

To read:
Find value on one scale. Read across or up to line, then read value off other scale.

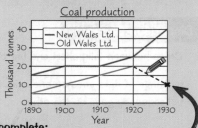

Coal production

Thousand tonnes

— New Wales Ltd.
— Old Wales Ltd.

1890 1900 1910 1920 1930
Year

To complete:
Find value on both scales. Mark 'x' where values meet. Join mark to line using ruler.

Scatter Graphs

Scatter graphs show the correlation between two things.

Positive

Negative

None

To read:
Look at graph's slope / angle & how close points are to line of best fit.
Close to line → strong correlation.
Far from line → weak correlation.

To add points:
Find value on both scales and mark where they meet.

Lines of best fit can extend outside data range to make predictions.

Relationship between altitude and rainfall

Rainfall / mm

Line of best fit

0   400   800   1200
Altitude / m

To draw line of best fit, draw roughly through middle of scattered points.

Geographical Skills

Charts and Graphs

Pie Charts

To find % for wedge:
- Use protractor to find angle of wedge.
- Divide by 360.
- Multiply by 100.

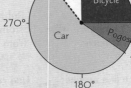

Pie Chart of Transport Type

324° 0°

Bicycle

270° — 90°

Car Pogostick

126°

180°

To draw wedge from %:
- Turn % into decimal.
- Multiply by 360.
- Draw wedge of that many degrees.

Whole pie = 360°

Protractor

Pro Tractor

To find amount wedge represents:
- Work out percentage.
- Turn percentage into decimal.
- Multiply decimal by total a full pie represents.

To draw wedge from amount:
- Divide amount by total a full pie represents.
- Multiply by 360.
- Draw wedge of that many degrees.

Dispersion Diagrams

Cross between tally chart and bar chart.

- **Range of data goes on one axis.** ➡
- **Frequency goes on the other.**

More dots in category = event more frequent.

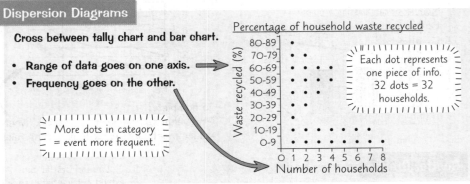

Percentage of household waste recycled

Each dot represents one piece of info. 32 dots = 32 households.

Waste recycled (%): 80-89, 70-79, 60-69, 50-59, 40-49, 30-39, 20-29, 10-19, 0-9

Number of households: 0 1 2 3 4 5 6 7 8

Population Pyramids

Show the population of a country by age and gender.

- **Horizontal axis — no. of people**
- **Vertical axis — age groups**
- **Left side — male population**
- **Right side — female population** ➡

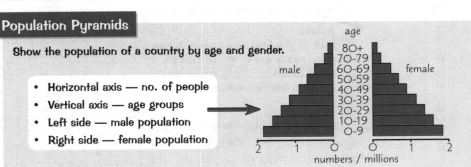

age

male   80+ 70-79 60-69 50-59 40-49 30-39 20-29 10-19 0-9   female

2 1 0   0 1 2

numbers / millions

Statistics

Definitions

Mode, median and mean = measures of average.

MODE
The most common number.

MEDIAN
The middle value (when in size order).

MEAN
The total of items ÷ the number of items. ➡ $798 ÷ 7 = 114$

e.g. 64   64   90   95   142   159   184

When there are two middle numbers, the median is halfway between the two.

RANGE
The difference between the highest and lowest number. ➡ $184 - 64 = 120$

LOWER QUARTILE
The value a quarter of the way through the ordered data.

MEDIAN

UPPER QUARTILE
The value three-quarters of the way through the ordered data.

e.g. 2   3   6   6   7   9   13   14   17   22   22

INTERQUARTILE RANGE
The difference between the upper quartile and the lower quartile. ➡ $17 - 6 = 11$

Percentages and Percentage Change

To find X as a percentage of Y:

1. Divide X by Y.
2. Multiply this number by 100.

E.g. This year, 35 out of 270 houses in Oldtown were burgled. Calculate the % of houses that were burgled.

To find 35 as a percentage of 270:

$$X ÷ Y × 100$$
$$35 ÷ 270 × 100 = 13\%$$

To calculate percentage change:

$$\text{percentage change} = \frac{\text{final value} - \text{original value}}{\text{original value}} × 100$$

A positive value shows an increase. A negative value shows a decrease.

E.g. Last year, only 24 houses were burgled. Calculate the percentage change in burglaries.

$$\frac{35 - 24}{24} × 100 = 46\% \text{ increase}$$

Acknowledgements

Data for causes of deforestation in the Amazon on page 13 from Mongabay.com.

Topographic map of the United Kingdom on page 19 by Captain Blood, Licensed under the Creative Commons Attribution-Share Alike 3.0 Unported license. https://creativecommons.org/licenses/by-sa/3.0/deed. en)

Photo on page 21 (Old Harry Rock) © Raymond Knapman. Licensed under the Creative Commons Attribution-Share Alike 2.0 Generic Licence. http://creativecommons.org/licenses/by-sa/2.0/

Photo on page 22 (aerial view of Alkborough Flats, 2007) © Chris. Licensed under the Creative Commons Attribution-Share Alike 2.0 Generic Licence. http://creativecommons.org/licenses/by-sa/2.0/

Data on the Oxford Flood Alleviation Scheme on page 27 © Crown copyright. Contains public sector information licensed under the Open Government Licence v3.0. https://www.nationalarchives.gov.uk/doc/open-government-licence/version/3/

Urban population data on page 31 source: United Nations Population Division. World Population Prospects: 2018 Revision. From The World Bank: World Development Indicators, licensed under the CC BY-4.0 License. https://creativecommons.org/licenses/by/4.0/

Birth rate data on page 31 source:
(1) United Nations Population Division. World Population Prospects: 2017 Revision.
(2) Census reports and other statistical publications from national statistical offices,
(3) Eurostat: Demographic Statistics,
(4) United Nations Statistical Division. Population and Vital Statistics Report (various years),
(5) U.S. Census Bureau: International Database, and
(6) Secretariat of the Pacific Community: Statistics and Demography Programme. From The World Bank: World Development Indicators, licensed under the CC BY-4.0 License. https://creativecommons.org/licenses/by/4.0/

Map symbols on page 57 and 58 © Crown copyright and database rights 2020 OS 100034841

Every effort has been made to locate copyright holders and obtain permission to reproduce sources. For those sources where it has been difficult to trace the copyright holder of the work, we would be grateful for information. If any copyright holder would like us to make an amendment to the acknowledgements, please notify us and we will gladly update the book at the next reprint. Thank you.